ON THE BEAT

Also by Guy Robin

Dysfunction
Indomitable

ON THE BEAT

Stories from Policing the streets of London in the 1980's.

GUY ROBIN

Copyright © 2024 by Guy Robin

All rights reserved.

ISBN: 979-8-3457-1173-6

No part of this publication may be reproduced, distributed, or transmitted in any form or by any means, including photocopying, recording, or other electronic or mechanical methods, without the prior written permission of the author, except as permitted by U.K. copyright law. For permission requests, contact Guy Robin.

For privacy reasons, some names, locations, and dates may have been changed.

To my wife Paula.

Foreword

While contemplating my formative years in the Metropolitan Police Force (it wasn't called a Service then) I decided to try and break down some of my memories and thoughts into brief four-line stanzas or prose. I have never had an opportunity to write poetry before, so thought I would try. I wanted to create something concise and pithy to get my feelings across. Some came to me quite quickly, but others were more difficult to construct.

I will provide each of the poems with some notes, a little explanation and context. I will also try and interpret some of the more colloquial words and expressions to assist understanding each poem. All the opinions expressed are mine. I didn't climb to the dizzy heights of senior management but I was witness to decisions and policies that I sometimes didn't agree with.

I hope you find these poems interesting, educational and thought provoking. I finished my 30 years in 2016 and I now watch from my retirement chair at the daily and serious challenges my colleagues within the service have to contend with. To all officers currently serving, you have my deepest and utmost admiration. I am not sure the job you do today is one that I could do. From the bottom of my heart, I thank you.

April 2024

Glossary of Terms

Body. Possibly means the deceased. More likely an arrested person.

Bugle. As in, to give it some 'bugle' when driving. To drive fast or quickly.

Ding Dong. Not a Leslie Phillips line, but a description of a serious fight or altercation.

Double Bubble. Earning twice your normal hourly or daily rate of pay.

Japscrackers. An expression describing a gentleman's penis and testicles.

L.O.B. Load of Bollocks. Given over the radio as the result of a call when there was no trace of said incident. Official terminology: Area search, no trace.

Manor. The area of London that you cover. Your ground, your patch, if you like.

Mumper or Blagger. An officer able to procure things at little or no expense.

Nads. Gonads or testicles.

Old Sweat/ Old Lag. Pretty much anyone who is not a Probationary Constable. Senior Constables and other officers with more than a few years' service.

One in the Bin. A person in custody at the police station.

Probbie. Probationary Constable. Probation lasts for two years, after that you are confirmed in the rank of constable.

Refs. Official refreshment breaks in the canteen.

Rubberneckers. Members of the general public, with no involvement in an incident, who are keen to view, get in the way and generally be a nuisance. More recently armed with mobile phones, but fortunately not in my day! Also, Disaster groupies.

Scrote. Similar to Wrongun. A criminal or villain. Quite likely used when discussing a prisoner or well-known felon.

The Nick. The police station, **Whisky Alpha**, sometimes also called **The Factory.**

Trap One. The first of a line of cubicles in a public toilet.

Wrongun. A criminal or villain. Someone not on the level or dishonest.

Introduction

I joined the Metropolitan Police Service on 24th February 1986. I was 20 years old and less than three years out of school. You could say my life experience was minimal. I'd always thought I would end up in the army, like my elder brother, but circumstance and timing changed my path to the police.

Hendon is where the Metropolitan Police Training school was situated in those days. The campus skyline was dominated by the accommodation tower blocks. I was allocated a room in the male block on the 11th floor, with a great view of Farrow House (communication training block) and an above ground section of the Northern Line.

The course at Hendon lasted twenty weeks. It consisted of regular assessments and exams about the law, practical tests to see how you deal with a variety of true-life scenarios and running endlessly around the 400 metres athletic track. Other tests of fitness followed. Your ability to swim, jump off the high board and countless team building exercises; probably designed to make you too tired to stay up late in the campus bar.

The training ended with a passing-out parade with lots of marching up and down. I don't think in the following thirty years of my service I ever marched anywhere again. We were also allocated the stations we were going to be joining. You could indicate which part of London you would like, but beyond that, it was out of your control. I plumped for South West London please? Thinking I might get the suburban delights of Wimbledon or perhaps Kingston. I got Battersea!

In addition to the allocation of a police station, there was the allocation of a room in the single persons accommodation or as they were known, "Section Houses". I was given a room on the first floor of Gilmore Section House, Renfrew Road, Kennington; just around the corner from the World-famous Oval Cricket Ground. Down a dingy corridor, my room consisted of a single bed, a built-in wardrobe, a sink with a mirror above it and a desk with a chair. The curtained window gave a spectacular view of the Lambeth Magistrates Court across the road. Ironically, if you have ever been in a prison cell it was about the same size. The interior was slightly less spartan and there was no wicket in the door! But beyond that.

Even though it was only a few miles, transport links between my new digs and Battersea Police Station were limited and once I joined a Relief, my starting and finishing times would fall outside public transport services. So, on a brief visit home to my mother, who lived in Dorset, I bought a Suzuki GP100 motorcycle. I roared back up to London. Along the A35, A31 and A3 on my new dream machine and secured parking for it in the basement of the Section House. On a good day I could get between Gilmore and the Nick in about six minutes. This trusty steed became my transport to and from work, at all times and in all weathers for the next few years.

Battersea Police Station was part of the Borough of Wandsworth, just south of the River Thames. The District was identified as W, with Wandsworth (WW), Tooting (WD) and Battersea (WA) being the main Divisional stations. Battersea Division itself, took the area immediately south of the river from Wandsworth Bridge in the west, to Vauxhall Bridge in the east and as far south as Clapham South tube on the Northern Line. Battersea Police Station was located at 118 Battersea Bridge Road. When I arrived there in 1986 it had just had a refurbishment to the interior, but the front of the building had been preserved the way that it had presumably always been. I think even today, after converting the station to a block of upmarket apartments, the front has been left pretty much as it was when I arrived on that sunny day in September 1986.

Before becoming a fully-fledged uniformed officer on the streets of London, you have to go through a ten-week street duties course. There were eight of us who joined Battersea Division. The course was run by a very experienced Sergeant and two equally experienced and a little world-wearier old lags called Bob and Alan. The idea is that they would effectively "puppy walk" you around the streets, taking calls and showing you how things are done. Every assignment resulted in a mountain of paperwork.

During the ten weeks we were faced with shoplifters, recording sudden deaths, domestic disturbances and any other disputes you can think of. Dealing with damage only and personal injury accidents (they were still called accidents then; with a nice, thick, Accident Reporting book to fill in). Reporting people for motoring transgressions like bus lanes, red lights and no left turns into Stanmer Street from Battersea Park Road (a personal favourite, because so many people did it and it was close to the Nick). These were in the days before fixed penalty notices and enforcement cameras appeared.

The eight of us completed the course. Some got to process more shoplifters, others dealt with more sudden deaths! Usually, it was just the luck of the draw on the day as to who was available when the calls came in. We each completed a record of work book to show that we'd had an opportunity to do a variety of different things. Suddenly before I knew it, the ten weeks were done and after a weekend off, I was due to join D Relief the following Monday. I'll be honest. It was quite a nervous weekend.

In the mid 1980's most, if not all stations, worked a four-Relief system. A very simple and straight forward shift pattern that included those oh-so-enjoyable quick change-overs. To explain. Start Night Duty at 10pm on a Monday, continue through that first week until 6am the following Monday morning. Back in at 2pm until 10pm that same Monday (8-hour quick change-over number one). A further late shift on Tuesday with Wednesday and Thursday off. Back in on Friday at 6am, the same on Saturday and Sunday. Monday and Tuesday off. Back in at 2pm on the Wednesday. Five of these 'Lates' until 10pm on the Sunday evening. Monday morning back in at 6am, that is quick change-over number two. Continue these early starts until finishing at 2pm on Thursday. The rest of the week and weekend off until back in at 10pm the following Monday evening. Then repeat. In my case for the next five years.

I was joining the Relief at 10pm that Monday evening, with a week of Night Duty stretched out before me. Nothing can prepare you for 'Nights'. Your body fights against staying awake right through the night. I felt constantly tired and a little bit 'spaced out'. Sleeping during the day is at best, fitful and you eat at strange times so your digestive system has difficulty too. Finishing at 6am I was always in a rush to get back to my Section House room, clamber into bed and fall asleep before the rest of the world woke up and disturbed me.

Suddenly, I was a fully-fledged police officer, PC 902 WA, now a member of D Relief.

Battersea Police Station. C 1905.

Poems

1	The Relief	9
2	Section House	17
3	Beat Duty (Early Turn)	27
4	Beat Duty (Late Turn)	43
5	Beat Duty (Night Shift)	57
6	Robbery	71
7	Notting Hill	77
8	Aid at Wapping	87
9	A Heston Rave	93
10	Whisky One	103
11	Railway!	129
12	Christmas Bereavement	143
13	Mortuary and a Jolly Jape!	157
14	Aid Opportunities	167
15	M. P. A. A. (Metropolitan Police Athletic Association)	189
16	Take His Arm!	199
17	The Jumper	209
18	Murder and Suicide	217
19	Officer Safety	225
20	And finally……… Trinity Road	237

The Relief

The boots on the ground that deal with it all.
The Sergeants run the show, with professional zeal.
About forty strong, until changes caused it to stall.
A powerful entity; to management, it didn't appeal.

A collection of characters with a multitude of skill sets.
Old sweats and Probbies sharing a shift.
A hierarchy of job allocation. I'm getting this one, I bet!
Feeling a part of something, give the spirits a lift.

The Relief at a station covers Earlies, Lates and Nights.
Hard working, hard playing; each of the four their own identity.
This collective. An amalgam of uniformed delights.
Proactive, reactive. An eight-hour rush, seldom sedentary.

A surrogate family. Supportive, instructive and fun.
Personal secrets, banter, wind ups and trauma support.
Uniform carriers will soon head for the sun.
Foolish managers try to interfere.
This knowledgeable experience can't be bought.

So, salute the grass roots, the humble lynch pin of the force.
Before loss of Heraldic crest and change to service.
Remember this finest working model; before a change. Of course.
Change for changes sake? We now pay the price.

In the introduction, I mentioned that at the end of all my training I joined D Relief at Battersea Police Station. One other new recruit joined with me, which eased some of the nerves. I was given a Reporting Sergeant, who supervised me for the next eighteen months of my probationary period (Probationary Officer = Probbie. Experienced Officer = Old Sweat). The Sergeants ran the show, with deft touches of acknowledgement to the Inspector, but it was the Sergeants who were in charge. Forty officers parading for Night Duty was about right at that time. It gradually dwindled over the years. Specialist units were formed, like the TSG (Territorial Support Group) and any number of other squads and collectives seemed to draw officers away from the Beat Duty Reliefs.

The beauty of this team was the merging of such a diverse talent pool, with some really experienced officers assisting to a greater or lesser extent, raw recruits like myself. As time passed and you work together and deal with some interesting and serious incidents, you obviously build a bond. You knew so much about each other. On a professional level you know who can do what, in a given situation and how they would react under pressure. As a young officer, I knew that I would get all the shitty calls. The several month-old sudden deaths. Every school crossing patrol. Standing on unsecure premises. All neatly and expertly choreographed by my excellent Reporting Sergeant.

But this group became family. They looked out for you when the job got tough. We socialised together and went on trips away. The camaraderie I felt on the Relief at Battersea was never replicated for the rest of my service. It wasn't for everybody, and those who couldn't quite gel tended to gravitate away from the Relief more quickly. It was a tough initiation. There were wind ups and jokes played on people. There was name calling, banter, some pretty dark humour and if you got a nickname it stuck. There are people on the Relief who I only knew by their nicknames, not sure if I could recall their real names, even now. But I always felt that it showed you had been noticed and had been welcomed.

On one occasion, I had gone to court with a Breach of the Peace the morning after a Night Duty and as a consequence, I was switched to a late shift on a Saturday night. This meant working with a different Relief. I spent the Saturday late shift with the fearsome C Relief. I don't know how it happened, but after refs I was posted as the operator on the station van. My driver was a terrifying, tall, dark-haired officer with as little as eight years' service, which to me, placed him in the 'Old Sweat' category.

He never spoke. He never looked at me. He just drove the van. I made a couple of attempts at conversation, but just received grunts in reply. I decided to hold my council. Our role was primarily for the transportation of prisoners. At this time the van was a Leyland Sherpa. Rear wheel drive, kitted out with bench seats down the sides of the rear, with a plywood bulkhead to protect the driver from whatever was sliding around in the back.

After about an hour of silently being driven around the streets of Battersea we were allocated a call to a disturbance outside the Gala Bingo Hall at the top end of Plough Road, where it meets St. John's Hill. I acknowledged receipt of the call and indicated we were on our way. My driver gunned the engine a little more, but we were by no means rushing to the scene. Finally, he spoke.

"Probably be all over by the time we get there. Just get out with me and follow my lead. OK?"

"Right", was all I could muster as a response.

On arrival we were confronted by eight to ten, fairly drunk ladies of indeterminate age, all shrieking and shoving each other. We got out and my driver walked up and grabbed one of the girls by the arm. Without looking, she swung around and caught him the most beautiful haymaker of a punch right on the bridge of his nose. It seemed to freeze the action amongst the group and put my driver on his backside. I froze too for a split second before grabbing this woman myself.

"You do not have to say….."

"What the fuck are you doing?" my resurrected driver had risen behind me, like some towering demonic figure and interrupted my cautioning of the young lady.

"She's mine. Open the back doors". And he then let out the most off-putting and slightly maniacal laugh (which has never really left me). He grabbed the perpetrator of the assault by the rear waistband of her jeans and the rear neck of her sweater and lifted her off the ground.

"You're nicked love" he grinned.

I hastily opened the doors of the van, just in time for my injured colleague to launch the arrested woman in. I did wonder if I hadn't been so quick with the doors, would he have waited with the throw? I was about to get in the back of the van with the woman when my bloodied driver slammed the doors.

"No! The first thing she'll do at the station is say you groped her. She'll be alright".

He turned to face the rest of the opened mouthed collection of rapidly sobering women and in what must have been his politest voice, bid them good night. We both got back in the van.

"Whisky Alpha, that disturbance at the Bingo. One in the back for assault. The rest given words of advice and sent on their way; we are now leaving the scene. Whisky Alpha Two, out".

And that was that. We were on our way back to the Nick with a prisoner.

When we got to the charge room and presented our prisoner to the Custody Sergeant, I stood waiting to hear my colleague give the evidence of the Actual Bodily Harm (ABH) committed on him. But instead, he simply gave evidence for a drunk and incapable and told the gaoler to put her in a detention room rather than a cell.

I have to admit I was confused. A little later, over a coffee in the canteen where we were writing up our notes, he explained. The assault had no intent. She was just scrapping. She was drunk, young and had been a bit stupid. She had hit him in the face, but no real harm done. It was just a cut not a broken nose. The newly formed Crown Prosecution Service (CPS) would certainly not take it forward as an ABH, most likely a common assault. So, all that paperwork for a poxy common assault. Also, if there was a charge, were we not giving a young girl a criminal record for an act of stupidity when under the influence?

You see, that is why the Reliefs mattered. You had these scary, but iconic characters imparting their wisdom to young impressionable 'Probbies' like me. I had been guided by one of the fiercest officers I had ever met. But inside, he had a heart and an intellect to try and do the right thing. I saw him in a different light after that evening. When later he was transferred to D Relief (I think the C Relief Inspector was scared of him too), I had great pleasure in once more working on numerous shifts with him. The laugh always remained strangely off-putting though.

To me, it all seemed to be working. We usually had enough troops on duty. Calls got answered, scrotes got nicked or at least squared up and there was even time for some proactive stuff, rather than just reactive. People could move on to other things because there were still huge numbers of recruits joining. The initiation into Relief working always meant that new officers were getting Policing 101 from seasoned officers. There was always a core of long serving, established officers content to hang around on the Relief. I imagine it was because they were satisfied. But as with everything, change happens. One senior officer gets a light bulb moment and dreams up Total Geographic or Sector Policing and another dreams up Inter Divisional Transfer or Tenure and it all came to an end.

Perhaps the power of the Relief was too daunting for senior officers? Perhaps it was deemed not cost effective to continue in this way? The shift pattern was certainly well outside of employment regulations and quite unhealthy, but I got used to it. When the Reliefs were broken up and replaced by the next thing, I was saddened. Working on D Relief for the first nine years of my service was without question, the best time of my thirty years. The friends I forged during that time remain with me now. The hard, sometimes relentless work, coupled with some banter and enormous fun was just how it was. Here's to The Reliefs. Enough said.

Section House

A small drab room, with a sink and a window.
A built-in wardrobe and a small creaky single bed.
An oblique view of the Magistrates Court below.
Communal washrooms and a canteen where we were fed.

Dingy low wattage bulbs light the long straight corridors.
A cell like space. Only the security flap in the door is missing.
A musty, over polished smell from the building's pores.
Constant alarm bells sounding and water pipes hissing.

When asleep off Nights I get rudely woken.
A firearms officer needs my room for a concealed position.
I dress quickly and shuffle down to the canteen. All chairs taken.
It's Court security when faced with IRA terrorism.

It was close to the station when duty called.
A six-minute ride on my Suzuki GP100.
Off duty and along the Walworth Road, I rolled.
Or perhaps the Elephant and Castle, where some fear to tread.

The Court Tavern opposite serving one of the finest lagers I've tasted.
Full to the brim with off duty cops and local nurses.
Many a night we would end up wasted.
Just as well, with a clear memory there could be so many more verses!

As a single person in the police, I was allocated a room in one of the Section Houses that used to exist throughout London. I didn't know it at the time, but I could have been sent to Nightingale Lane, Sylvan Hill, or possibly the one behind Tooting Police Station. But I got Gilmore House. A large, six storey office block type structure in Renfrew Road, Kennington, right opposite Lambeth Magistrates Court.

Gilmore was run by an amiable Sergeant at the time, but the role was civilianised shortly after my arrival. For the princely sum of £4 per month, I was given a single room on the first floor. It was well worn and basic. In need of a lick of paint and some homely touches to make it look a little less institutional. The majority of my meagre belongings were made up of my freshly issued Metropolitan Police uniform. Most of this I would decant to my station in due course.

There was a sink in the corner, with an unlit mirror above. No en-suite facilities, just some communal washrooms at the end of the corridor. A pair of flip-flops were quickly purchased for the daily shuffle to have a shower, use the heads, etc. No kitchenette; a ground floor canteen that served from about 8am to 7pm if you were lucky. There was a basement gym, with some free weights and a rickety old multigym set up. A couple of venerable old washing machines and a tumble dryer that was always broken. After a short while I found a launderette in the Walworth Road and paid the nice lady to do me a service wash. From the basement there were some doors out to the rear yard. A small space, not big enough for any cars (well, except the Sergeant's), but sufficient for my motorbike.

I bought myself a small, portable colour television. I imagine Gilmore, with its 200 plus rooms had about 200 plus televisions. All on the one licence! I remember walking around my local area. God it was grim. The Elephant and Castle shopping Mall. What a dump! I watched the film "Highlander" at the cinema there. I'd never go there now; too scared! The Walworth Road. A long snaking highway of shops and businesses, a bustling market and Carter Street Nick.

I only had a provisional licence, so rode my motorbike on L plates. I decided to use some of my rest days to learn to drive. I found the BSM driving centre down at the bottom end of the Walworth Road. My instructor was Earl. Perhaps the coolest man I had ever met. My overwhelming memory of Earl was his constant encouragement of,

"More gas, man, more gas", entreating me in his languid West Indian tone to move the Mini Metro a little faster as we negotiated traffic in that part of London. I passed my test first time in August 1987. Hard to believe that four years later I would get to be an Advanced Police Driver. But more of that later.

One of the strange quirks about Gilmore was what occurred during Court security at the Magistrates opposite. Lambeth Court was used for the first appearance of IRA terrorists. When such an appearance was scheduled, all cars in Renfrew Road had to be removed. Bicycles were not allowed to be left against railings and any that were, had their locks cut and were taken away. Armed officers naturally swarmed over the Court and surrounding area, which included Gilmore. It only happened to me once off Night

Duty. An armed officer knocked on my door, waking me from my deep 'off Nights' sleep. He regarded me with complete distain and explained he needed my room as a vantage point overlooking the Court building and road in front of it. I rose, put on my dressing gown and shuffled off to the canteen where several other similarly unimpressed probationary officers sat shivering in their pyjamas.

I changed rooms about three days later. Apparently, this was a 'jolly jape' by the amiable Sergeant, to place new recruits in these 'Vantage Point 'rooms! Thanks. I'm glad they civilianised him!

Perhaps the greatest saving grace of living at Gilmore was the public house opposite. The Court Tavern, as you would expect, was right next to Lambeth Magistrates Court. During the day, it was filled with solicitors, barristers, councillors for the prosecution (never the defence) and officers required at Court that day. In the evening it was crammed with the residents of Gilmore and nurses from several of their accommodation blocks at the end of the road, as St. Thomas' Hospital was no more than a stone's throw away.

It was where I got a taste for Hurlimann (Hooligan) Lager. A smooth, creamy pint with a hoppy after taste. I think it was about 4.8% ABV. A couple of pints of this and you knew you'd had a drink. On the third, I might pluck up the courage to talk to a nurse and by the end of the fourth I was asleep!

Gilmore was also close to Kennington Tube Station, on the Northern Line. This was in the days before automatic barriers and Oyster cards and the police were granted free travel on buses and tubes. Just flash your brief (Warrant Card) to the guard as you entered and exited the station. Four stops to the West End. A chance to see Top Gun, with some young actor called Tom Cruise, in one of the big cinemas, with the Dolby Stereo that made the building shake. All of this fun and games on my rest days, however, was short lived. Within a few months of joining D Relief, I got to know the score. Overtime!

In those days you could pretty much guarantee that three or four of your rest days could be worked for overtime. Over eight days' notice was at the time and a half rate. But less than eight! Double bubble; kerching! Thank you very much. Even as a non-skilled, non-driving probationer I could get overtime. Usually someone was on strike. Prison Officers or Ambulance crews and there were always prisoners housed at South Western Magistrates Court and in the vacant cells at Lavender Hill Police Station, which was next door. There was always security for something. Vulnerable witnesses or prisoners at New Malden. Aid to various parts of London. My favourite was Wapping after they stopped throwing stuff. I very quickly understood that the Duties Sergeant needed to know who you were and frequent visits to emphasise your availability would pay dividends; well double time usually.

One early opportunity for me was the London ambulance strike, which lasted from September 1989 until February 1990. This overtime tour of duty began in the canteen at Battersea Police Station. The army had been called in with a selection of ancient Land Rover ambulance conversions, top speed of about 35mph. They would post the driver and a medic and my role was navigator. We would have a quick debrief with the previous shift and then call Scotland Yard, using the suitcase sized 'portable' radio, confirming that we were available for deployment. When a call was received, I would sit up front with the driver and navigate us to the location of the person needing an ambulance. It was "Fred Karno's Circus" on most days. The main stumbling block to us providing a professional service to the public was the lack of equipment, especially for carrying patients. Most of the time we had to make do with a metal-framed collapsible chair. You've probably seen them; the metal is a cream colour and the fabric of the seat is burgundy. It folds flat and has tiny little wheels at the bottom. When the patient is on it you were supposed to lean it back gently and wheel the person about on it. Fucking useless!

One incident that sticks in my mind was while covering the Night shift. The call came in at about 11pm to a male having a suspected heart attack in a block of flats in Battersea High Street. The block was a tower of twelve storeys. We drove there hoping he'd be in a ground floor flat. Ha! Not a chance. He was on the 8th floor and had collapsed while he was on the toilet, so was lying on the bathroom floor with his pyjamas sort of half on and half not. Our patient was also, I estimated, to be in excess of twenty stone in weight. When we arrived at the foot of the tower block we pressed for the lift. It was smaller than a phone box inside and only one of us plus the collapsible chair thing could fit in it, so the army driver and I walked up the stairs as the medic ascended in the lift.

By the time the two of us walking up the stairs had got to the 8th floor we were both blowing a bit. Our medic colleague had got the patient into the recovery position, found a pulse and established the chap was breathing.

"He needs to go to hospital", from the medic.

"Ok, shall we put him on the chair?" my driver replied. He was ahead of me and I could see him working out the logistics and physics of getting a twenty-stone chap on to the chair, then into the dumb waiter pretending to be a lift.

We managed to give the man some dignity and got his pyjamas back on. Unfortunately, that was pretty much where the dignity ended. The three of us, using every ounce of strength we possessed got him on the chair, but he wasn't really on it. Perhaps one cheek of his capacious backside was on it, but when I took a step back it looked like he'd absorbed it.

The three of us carried, manhandled and dragged him out of the flat to the 8th floor landing and pressed for the lift. When the doors opened it was immediately obvious that in his recumbent position on the chair he would not fit. Fuck it! Now what?

We had abandoned the possibility of standing him up in the lift and letting him go down on his own. He was unconscious, it just didn't feel right. The only solution was to use the stairs. All eight flights of them. If we left him sitting on the chair it would mean lifting him down every single step. I didn't think that would be possible. It was then that I had a thought, inspired by the 1984 film, Greystoke: Legend of Tarzan. There is a scene in the film where the elderly Lord Greystoke, played by the brilliant and irascible actor Ralph Richardson, climbs to the top of the stairs of his grand stately home with a large silver tray. He then sits on the tray and shuggles his way to the edge of the top step, then, Cresta Run style, down he goes. Bumpety, bumpety, bumpety, bump!

"What? Slide him down eight flights of stairs?", the medic was clearly a bit doubtful of my suggestion.

"If we take him off the chair, fold it flat, strap him to it, then it becomes a sort of luge and we gently lower him down each flight to the turn on the stairs and then down to the lower floor", I was making it up as I went along, but it seemed to convince the army types.

Working as quickly as we could, we got the chap off the chair, folded it flat, turned it upside down, so the wheels were off the ground and wouldn't hinder the sliding. We strapped him back on to what was now just a metal frame and pushed him to the edge. The idea was that we would tilt the thing until gravity took over, but the three of us would hold on, to arrest the speed.

Utter bollocks! The moment we got him past the point of no return we just couldn't hold him and he slide down the stairs like a fat missile, crashing into the wall at the midway point. Quick as a flash we just lined him up for the next flight and repeated the process and just let him go. Eventually we got him into the ambulance, still breathing, still with a pulse. I got us allocated to St. Thomas' Hospital and off we went. Revving the nads out of the Land Rover the driver got 40mph out of it on parts of the journey. On arrival at the A and E, nurses appeared with a proper bed to transport the patient and our mountain of a man disappeared inside. We followed slowly behind to find a vending machine and a hasty coffee, before declaring to the Yard we were free for another call.

The doctor came out and spotted us. It's worth noting that this was the days before defibrillators became common place

"That chap you just brought in. His hearts going well. It's like he was given an almighty jolt by something. Did you drop him perhaps?"

"It was a little bit bumpy getting him down to the ground floor", the medic was the only one who could answer. The army driver and I were too busy choking on our coffee.

The man from the tower block in Battersea High Street survived his heart attack and his brush with the police and army ambulance crew!

So, despite on paper having eight rest days a month, the reality was I worked four of them and I was probably working the least compared to some. This did lead to me eating, breathing and living being a police officer. Very little time to have any sort of social life outside of work. It was therefore natural to socialise with your work colleagues and spend a good hour after shift in the Union Arms across the road from Battersea Station. Licensing hours were somewhat stricter then, but The Union Arms would usually be open and stay open, as long as there were coppers drinking there.

All this leads me very nicely to the different shifts we all worked, while conducting our beat duties on the Relief.

Beat Duty (Early Turn)

Up at Five; a ten-minute drive.
Locker room change, parade with appointments at six.
Patrols allocated, radio check, going live.
Out on my beat, tunic button missing, note to self, to fix.

A few hours of bus lane process near Chelsea Bridge.
Quota complete. A slow walk back in for refs.
Canteen banter can be close to the edge.
A breakfast fry up, followed by a report writing sesh!

Visiting the CAD room is rewarded with a MISPER enquiry.
An elderly relative not answering her phone.
A thirty-minute walk to a building by the library.
That familiar musty odour. Dead in her chair; sadly alone!

Stay on scene, get the doctor on way.
Big Tony from CID cleared it as natural causes.
Message sent to inform a nephew called Ray.
Remain at address until Late shift relieve, the controller chooses.

Just an hour late off, missed the first round at the pub.
Sniffing my clothes; can't get rid of the smell of death.
Tomorrow an appointment at the mortuary; there's the rub.
Another typical day on duty, no time to take a breath.

I was late for duty twice in my 30 years of service. On consecutive days, both Early Turn. On the first occasion I rolled in at about 6.20am. My Inspector sat me down in the canteen and gave me my one warning. "It happens; don't be late again".

The following day I once again raced up the back stairs at about 6.05am to be met at the door by my smiling Inspector. "Thank you for joining us officer, but I think you will find that you are incredibly early for Late Turn. Re-parade at 2pm. I will ensure that the Late Turn Inspector knows to expect you."

With that he walked off towards the Control Room. I went back to the Section House, to return for a Late shift and an extra quick change over the following morning. I was never late for duty again. It's probably why I am never late for anything, even if I sometimes turn up an hour early.

6am, though. It is early, but in my opinion preferable to when they changed the start time to 7am. In London that hour between 6am and 7am makes a massive difference to traffic, so the journey in was much easier. The Relief could parade, have a briefing, cup of tea and banter all before anybody else was moving about. Plus, your finish time was 2pm. This meant that there was still an afternoon available if you needed to do anything besides sloping off to the Union Arms for a couple of hours drinking. I will concede that it did have a cumulative effect and by the end of the fourth Early on the Thursday afternoon I was pretty tired.

Every Relief had a tea club. Its own locker full of coffee, tea, biscuits, sugar, usually expanding to bread for toast on Earlies, so there would also be butter, jam, marmalade and sometimes marmite, with a plentiful supply of milk in the fridge. The milk was blagged from the milk distribution dairy down at Nine Elms Lane. The Night Duty left one or two fresh newspapers acquired from the Menzies warehouse in Hester Road. All in all, the Reliefs were more than self-sufficient when the canteen was closed.

After parade there was an unwritten twenty minutes of tea and banter in the canteen before rolling out on to the streets. Sometimes the Sergeants had to cajole us out, especially in winter when it was still dark and raining. As a young probationer I was given a beat to patrol on foot. Most often on my own. Me against the world. Armed with a light-weight wooden truncheon secreted down the back of my trouser leg, a radio, whistle and a notebook. Beat Duty uniform was a crisp and pressed white shirt, with clip on tie, a four-button tunic and matching heavy trousers. You provided your own footwear and most gravitated to a pair of Doc Marten's or latterly some Magnum Hi Tec boots. Topped off by the traditional Beat Duty Policeman's helmet, providing neither protection from the elements or assault, but it was traditional and made you look the part, especially if you were short!

The Storno radios kind of worked. There were always blackspots and the batteries were notoriously short lived. Radio dialogue was always a hoot. You did a course at Hendon on radio protocol. Accuracy, brevity and speed (I still remember it over 35 years later). You were also conversant with the Phonetic Alphabet; or at least most of it.

"Whisky Alpha receiving, 902, over".

"902, go ahead, over"

"Can I have a vehicle check, Chelsea Bridge, over".

"Go ahead, over".

"It's Whisky Bingo, Uniform, One two, three, Y Yankee, over"

There was then a slight pause until the professional Controller came back.

"902, can you confirm. Whisky, BRAVO, Uniform, one two three Yankee, over".

And everyone could hear on the open channel the whole control room and rest of the Relief laughing as he corrected my mistake.

Happy days. I hastily brushed up on my phonetic alphabet.

After a few days on my first Early shifts patrolling my allocated beat, I quickly worked out a routine. With the onset of winter, my Beat Duty raincoat was not cutting it as insulation against the elements. For some reason when uniform was being issued I was given a short, thickly padded coat with silver buttons known as a 'Car Coat' and a full-length version. The full-length version was like wearing a padded suit you see a handler wearing when they let a police dog go crazy and savage them. I never wore that one. The car coat came in handy when it was really cold, but management hated 'silver buttons' for some reason and wouldn't let us wear it or got upset when they caught us wearing it.

Anyway, I digress. In the absence of a decent warm coat, patrolling on Earlies in winter was COLD. So, remembering my street duties I decided to find some unsuspecting motorists and report them for traffic offences. Traffic lights needed two of you, so, if patrolling in pairs, we could spot and stop for each other. My main junction for this was Latchmere Road, heading North across Battersea Park Road into Battersea Bridge Road. It was a short phase and in the rush hour people couldn't help themselves and on virtually every phase someone would cross the junction when the signal was red. I would be standing in Latchmere Road, with a good view (clear and unobstructed view actually) about 50 yards south of the junction with Battersea Park Road. I was watching for cars travelling north from me and across the traffic light-controlled junction. When a motorist failed to stop at a red signal, I would radio my colleague, who was positioned up near The Duke of Cambridge pub, in Battersea Bridge Road. He would stop the offending motorist and ask them to wait for me to join them. I would point out the offence, listen to the excuses, apologies, anger and abuse, then report them.

Unfortunately, more often than not I was patrolling alone, so I planned for my winter Earlies. After the obligatory tea and piss taking I made sure I had my notebook, a handful of process reporting books and most importantly a Home Office Road Traffic Form 1 (HO/RT 1). Most of the information needed to complete a thorough Process Report Book could be gleaned from a correctly filled in HO/RT 1. This was the legendary 'producer', given at the roadside if a motorist didn't have their driving licence, certificate of insurance and MOT with them. The person being issued had seven days from midnight of that day to produce their driving documents at a station of their choosing. This was all in the days before photo ID card driving licenses and computer linked centrally networked insurance and MOT information.

Armed with my forms and reporting books I left the Nick. I took a slow walk up to Parkgate Road and ambled along to Albert Bridge Road with the entrance to the park opposite. Battersea Park was an oasis of trees and gardens. You could walk along by the embankment and forget you were in London. Then drift past the Peace Pagoda and briefly wonder what it's all about. I kept going until I reached the other side of the park at the Chelsea Bridge entrance, just south of the bridge itself. The entrance provided a good little makeshift lay by where I could discuss things with stopped motorists. I was stopping cars for using the bus lane between 7am and 10am. This particular bus lane ran pretty much from Queen's Circus all the way to the other side of the bridge. There was an endless line of drivers who thought nothing of tearing up the inside lane to make progress on their way to work. In the days before cameras policed them, it was left to freezing probationary constables like me to monitor and enforce the rules. The beauty of this position was that you had an uninterrupted view down the arrow straight street, but could secret yourself just by the park entrance so that you couldn't be seen by a motorist until it was too late.

I would enforce this for about an hour, unless I got called to deal with something else. As a foot patrolling officer on the first half of Early Turn, you were left to manage your patrol as you saw fit. The hour or so I spent at Chelsea Bridge usually produced four or five people to be reported "for the question to be considered of prosecuting them" for the bus lane offence. As a police officer I could report them, but the decision to prosecute was taken by the administrative department where I submitted my reports, which was upstairs at the Station. A slow walk back through the park and a return to the station for my 9am refreshment break.

Refreshment breaks were forty-five minutes, which extended to an hour, unless something happened. Frequently a call would come over the radio for assistance in one capacity or another. When that happened the canteen, full of the entire section of the Relief on their break would empty, as they raced to help. Half eaten breakfasts and mugs of tea were abandoned in situ. Non-Relief personnel very quickly learned not to get in the way of a herd of charging officers answering a shout!

When not charging out to assist a colleague, I would usually sit down to a hearty cooked breakfast. While quite new in my service the canteens in the Met. started offering a '999' full cooked English breakfast, with accompanying choice of hot drink and toast. Once I had eaten and been put straight on all the letters of the phonetic alphabet, I could settle in and write out my report books. When complete, they had to be counter signed by my Reporting Sergeant. He ran on the 10p a mistake rule. It was important to make sure your notes and reports were completed correctly. Quite right! Months later when there was the possibility that some misguided motorist decided to 'give it a run' at Court you might have to read these scribblings out in open court about something that you could barely remember. Notes were always important and they have become ever more so now.

Once my reports had passed muster (usually about 50-90p's worth of mistakes that bolstered the Widows and Orphans Fund) I got into the habit of visiting the control room. I could sometimes get a chance to see which job I might get allocated or get a chance to choose between jobs. It didn't always work. Time it wrong and you could end up with all sorts of grief.

Some days the Section Sergeant would post me to a different beat, where the possibility of reporting motorists for offences would not be available. On one such cold, frosty morning I was patrolling Vicarage Crescent heading down towards Battersea High Street. It would have been about 7.30 – 8am, not completely daylight in the early winter. It was a quiet day, but down towards the High Street I could hear shouting. A dust cart was parked in Battersea High Street, right by the junction with Shuttleworth Road. I could see a man in high visibility clothing standing by the vehicle looking down at something lying in the road. As I got closer I could see it was an elderly female.

I rushed over to the scene, radioing in that I appeared to have an elderly female injured in the street and requested an ambulance.

"I just never saw her, my mates shouted for me to stop, but I didn't react in time", the high- viz wearing dustcart driver blurted out.

I took stock and knelt down next to the lady and felt for a pulse on her wrist. Nothing. I got my head down to her mouth and listened to see if I could hear or feel any breath coming from her. Again nothing. I am not a doctor, but I am pretty sure she was dead.

Suddenly more shouting. "Oh, it's my mum, oh God". Clearly the elderly lady lived close by and someone had got hold of her family. I was now crowded in my endeavours by a daughter, a couple of grandchildren and other 'rubberneckers' keen to see a dead pensioner.

"Whisky Alpha, how long for the ambulance, 902, over".

"902, five minutes, Whisky Alpha, over"

"Received, she has serious chest injuries, and is not breathing, 902, over.

"902, Whisky One on way to you". Ah! That's nice. Always reassuring to have other units with you to fend off a crowd.

Realising the crowd had heard me on the radio, I knew I had to do something.

I began trying to do some rudimentary Cardiopulmonary Resuscitation (CPR), beginning with the chest compressions. As I paced my palm heels on her sternum and began to do the compressions, I could feel that I was actually touching the surface of the road through her body. It quickly became apparent that the dust cart had completely flattened her chest area. But I had a family watching me, so I had to do something.

Fortunately, Whisky One and the Governor arrived and got the crowd back, took details of the driver and other witnesses, leaving me to give the body as much dignity as I could manage. Then the ambulance crew arrived.

"You know she's dead, right?" one of the paramedics stated.

"Yes", I whispered, "But that's her family over there, talking to my colleagues and I just couldn't stand here and do nothing".

"Ok, we'll take it from here, thanks", and they did the same as me, put in a breathing tube, got her on to a gurney and quickly into the back of the ambulance. The Duty Officer cleared me from the scene and I jumped in the back of the ambulance and off we went to St. George's Hospital, Tooting.

The elderly lady, Iris, was pronounced dead upon arrival at the hospital. A traffic skipper attended the scene and began his investigation. It transpired that it was one of those awful one-in-a-million type calamitous accidents. Iris had been on her way down to the shops to get some milk and a newspaper for herself. She was walking down Shuttleworth Road. When she reached the junction with Battersea High Street, she went to cross the road, directly in front of the dustcart, intending to continue along Battersea High Street, towards the area where the shops are. At the moment she stepped off the pavement, the stationary dustcart moved off to continue its collection. Why didn't the driver see Iris, as she crossed in front of his vehicle? The clue was her height. Iris was only 4 foot 10 inches tall.

As she stepped off the curb into the road, she passed immediately in front of the truck. From the driver's seat, despite the elevated position, he couldn't see Iris, because she was too short to be seen above the windscreen. She passed directly below it, making her invisible to him. She had no idea that the truck was about to move off. One of the dustmen collecting the bins turned to see this tragedy unfolding and shouted for the driver to stop. To make matters worse, having driven over Iris with the front wheels of the truck, as a result of the shouts from the other dustman, he reacted by reversing the truck back over her again. This was what I chanced upon, as I walked down Vicarage Crescent that morning.

In between patrolling the streets, the other type of duty given to a new probationary officer would be Station Officer. In those days we had civilian support staff, who worked in some of the administrative offices or answered the phones, but the Station Officer role was still conducted by a police officer. Your job was to deal with customers at the front counter. Members of the public might wander in with items of property, dogs or anything else they had found, requiring form filling and receipt writing. People clutching their HO/RT1 stubs with all their driving documents to be checked. Persons on bail signing in, as part of their conditions of release. Any number of other visitors attending the station; solicitors, appropriate adults, social services, council officials. All to be greeted by me, as the Station Officer. There were other duties to attend to at the Front office too. Internal correspondence had to be sorted and placed in the correct pigeonhole, eight Smith and Wesson pistols in the safe had to be checked and the ammo counted, radio batteries needed charging and finally you had to make tea for the Communications staff and the Custody Sergeant. Performing this task became less frequent once the civilian staff were rolled out, but it was a useful way, as a young officer, to learn how a police station worked. It got me used to writing reports, filling in forms and making tea at an early stage of my service.

A common type of call for a non-driving, foot-duty, beat cop like me, would be a MISPER (Missing Person). The station would receive notification that there had been no contact with an elderly relative for some time. The caller wouldn't live locally and their nearest and dearest would live somewhere on our Manor. My probationary colleagues and I would be the most likely to be given these calls.

About the fifth MISPER call I was given was not the usual L.O.B! (Load of Bollocks). The enquiry had come from a concerned son called Ray, who lived down in the Kent countryside somewhere. He hadn't been able to get a reply on the phone from his mum, who lived halfway up a tower block called Castlemaine, south of Battersea Park Road. Upon arrival I was heartened to see that the lifts were working. The address was on the 12th floor. As the lift doors opened on that floor, I was confronted with what would become, an all too familiar smell of moulding decay that just stuck in the back of your throat. There were several items of junk mail jammed in the letter box. I cleared these and lifted the flap and peered in. The smell was palpable and obvious. I radioed in my discovery and thoughts. The controller called back to say the son had advised that a key could be found on top of the door lintel. I reached up and sure enough a brass Yale key was resting there. I opened the door and walked in, trying to avoid the flies buzzing around everywhere. I was drawn to the front room of the small flat. Sat in the chair, decaying peacefully was Ray's mother.

This was the second dead body I had ever seen. My first was on the street duties course. I was sent to another old lady's flat on the Patmore Estate. She had been found dead in bed by her neighbour.

A helpful CID officer took me through my role to search the flat and have a close look at the body to establish if anything might be considered suspicious. This might require moving the body and my friendly CID colleague prepared me for the disquieting releases of air from a body when it is moved. But as the lady on the Patmore had only recently been seen by her doctor it was a very straight forward case of waiting for the hospital to send a wagon to take the body to the hospital.

My lady at Castlemaine had been there, the doctor reckoned, for about a week to ten days. This was not uncommon. I recall other bodies that had gone undiscovered for months. One in particular which fascinated the attending doctor, was due to the underfloor heating system having dried and mummified the body in the months it had been there.

Sometimes it might take a great deal of searching to see if there was anything or anyone to find. I was called to another flat due to a foul smell. Upon gaining entry, the place was a tip. There was rubbish piled up everywhere. Old takeaway food containers abandoned on the floor. Black bin bags piled high in every room and new walls created entirely by stacked newspapers. It was hard to move around without stepping on something dreadful. The dark sticky carpet was actually shimmering with cockroaches. Eventually my luck ran out and I discovered an ancient carton of milk with my size 10. The carton had expanded with age and as I put my weight on it. Bang! It exploded upwards covering my trousers and tunic in a fetid splat of curdled milk. After all that, I didn't find anything suspicious or a dead body in that place. Just a trip to see the Property Officer for some replacement items of uniform! Officially replacement uniform could be obtained from one of the mobile clothing vans that did the rounds of the Divisions, but they were few and far between. Your best bet was the Battersea Property Officer, who was like the King Rat character James Clavell wrote about. If you wanted something, pop down to the Property Office and he'd set you straight, for a minimal donation to….? yep you guessed it, The Widows and Orphans Fund!

On this particular occasion at Castlemaine, I called the CID requesting them to attend, called for a doctor to certify life extinct. It's one of those things that requires a doctor to certify. He's the expert and despite my 'body' being a blueish grey colour I was not considered an expert in the eyes of the law to be able to say that Ray's mum was dead, officially.

When all these things had been put in place and a call had been made for the hospital to collect the body I found out the expected news. There would be a delay in the pick-up. I should remain on scene until further notice. If the delay dragged into the next shift, then someone from that Relief would attend to take over. The usual casually late finish, not really enough to claim any overtime, just late off! After writing a few notes for the following mornings declaration to the hospital pathologist (continuity) I basically sat down on the sofa opposite Ray's dead mum, now known to me as Irene, put the telly on and waited for someone from Late Turn to appear.

Very much like our own start, the next Relief would have their briefing followed by a round of tea and banter before heading out on patrol. All this led to me being stood down at about 2.30pm. The Late Turn van driver had dropped my replacement off and very kindly waited to give me a lift back to the station. By the time I had got my notes signed and handed back my radio it was close to 3pm before I got across the road to The Union Arms, where my team were almost through their second round. As I sat down in my half blues with a pint, I could still smell that awful musty odour of death. It clings to everything; gets into the very fibres of the clothes you are wearing. Even washing them doesn't remove it. Everything I had on would be binned and I'd have to make another trip to the Property Office. Enough for today. Back in the pub it was my round because I was late off.

Beat Duty (Late Turn)

Late shift parades at Two in the afternoon.
I get given a crime report, MISPER and a school crossing patrol.
Walking the beat alone, reports completed, the crossing patrol starts soon.
The youngsters cross. An hour of proper hand signals takes its toll.

The report and enquiry written and logged, time to grab a bite.
The choice of a shoplifter at Boots or kids playing on the railway?
I take the kids. Less grief! Then picked up by the van, as it is light.
Area search no trace re the kids; we took two alarm calls on way.

Keep operating on the van. Transport a drunk and incapable.
Hose out the back, then back out on the streets.
Take a shout! Chasing suspects St. John's Hill, Whisky One unable.
Lost towards the Winstanley. We spot a wrongun; see who he meets.

A red-light runner stopped; no attitude so verbally warned, not reported
Refuel the van at Queen's Circus, then trawl the back streets, on alert.
Two likely lads stopped and searched, out of the area escorted.
A sudden cry for urgent assistance. Gun the engine before anyone gets hurt.

Find our colleague outside the Butchers Arms, fight inside in progress.
We wait for more units to arrive. We enter stick drawn, utter carnage.
We start cracking heads, avoiding flying furniture and ejecting patrons.
So many to nick and particulars recorded; now survey the damage!

Getting into the station for a 2pm start, always took longer than in the morning. I could usually still make good time, weaving through the traffic at Vauxhall Cross and along Nine Elms Lane, past the (then) derelict Battersea Power Station and Dogs Home. With a motorbike I could also park in the yard, unlike the car owners who had limited options in Hyde Lane or they could take their chances on the Surrey Lane Estate and possibly come back to a car on bricks.

It was the busy shift. You always arrived, had a briefing, a quick brew and hit the ground running. Very little time for a catch up with colleagues. It was straight out on the beat, clearing calls that had come in as the Reliefs changed over. There was usually a burglary to report or a theft from a motor vehicle to deal with. In those days we would attend the scene, speak with the victim and take as many details as possible. Learn as much about points of entry for the burglary, anything that might link this one with the numerous others. Get as much of a description about stolen items, include serial numbers and distinguishing marks. Above all, try and show empathy and compassion with the invariably traumatised victim. Give them a reference for their insurance company and explain that a Crime Prevention Officer would be in touch.

These were the days before computers could process crime statistics in a second. The Crime Desk had these huge binders, where all the hand-written crime reports were collated and logged and given a running number. This was the number the victim needed for their insurance company. The Crime Desk would decide if a lowly probationary constable like myself would be allocated a crime to investigate or, more usually, it would be passed across to a CID officer. Like every report, it would be poured over with a keen eye to ensure it was completed correctly and all necessary fields had been marked. Crime reports could take a while.

There were numerous school crossing patrols dotted around the area. If a 'lollypop' lady was ill or absent it was invariably a probationer who would take over the role. Try to instil a bit of road sense into clueless kids and their mothers, all the while making sure to give hand signals in the Highway Code approved manner. It has always struck me as odd that when women with prams cross the road, they always push the pram out into the road first? Giving hand signals in the approved manner is incredibly tiring after a while, too. The saving grace was they only lasted thirty minutes to an hour and then you could return to the station to write up your reports and result your enquiries.

Refs were taken at either 5pm or 6pm and the canteen usually had some decent hot food to choose from. This was a chance to catch up with colleagues over a cup of tea and a meal. The Duty Sergeant could have some information to share and very occasionally you might get posted to something other than foot patrol. It wasn't uncommon to be posted to one of the vehicles after refs. Most vehicles would patrol the latter half of Late shift with an operator. It was likely that a probationer would get the van (Whisky Alpha Two) rather than the more glamourous Area Car (Whisky One).

There were always shoplifters to deal with. A right pain in the arse, requiring a full file of case papers. You knew that dealing with a shoplifter could easily take the whole shift, especially if they wanted a solicitor. If there was anything else to deal with, I'd prefer that, over a shoplifter please.

Now it just so happened that slap bang in the middle of our ground was Clapham Junction railway station. I know it's called Clapham Junction, yet it's in the middle of Battersea; I never found out why that was. It was one of the busiest stations and marshalling yards in the country. There were also loads of smaller branch lines squirrelling their way through the ground too. The railway lines certainly caused us more problems than the river. There were always reports of people and things on the line, suspects would use it as a route to evade capture when being chased and it was a popular location for suicides. It was also where the Clapham Rail Crash happened in 1988. More of which later.

Drunks on the whole, were a fairly harmless bunch. Most of the time they were simply arrested for their own safety and welfare. A few hours or a night in the cell, being monitored by the gaoler, before being released in the morning, when sober. No caution, no criminal record, just a place of safety. Unfortunately, a drunk and incapable in the van might sometimes vomit or worse in the back and after having got him or her into a cell back at the station, guess who would be the one tasked with cleaning out the interior of the vehicle?

While I was busy cleaning, my 'old sweat' driver would probably be waiting with a cup of tea. It was just the way of things. A vehicle would always be left at the end of the shift with a full tank of fuel. Drivers could fill up at a petrol station using an agency card or sometimes they might travel across to Lambeth, where a Met. Police premises had its own petrol pumps. As the late shift wore on and darkness fell there would sometimes be an opportunity to cruise down the back streets and see what was about.

Battersea had areas of great wealth and poverty right next to each other, so to the criminally minded there were rich pickings to be had. I very quickly learnt that it was advantageous to patrol certain streets to easily spot those who simply didn't fit. I sometimes found myself being driven around in the van with a colleague, who only had two or three years more service than me, but he had a knack for spotting a wrongun. You would stop a couple of likely lads in Lurline Gardens around the back of the Mansion blocks on Prince of Wales Drive and if you were lucky, there might be something on them that would give sufficient grounds to arrest. Failing that, you were dealing with scrotes and a thorough stop and search would finish with some words of advice and then follow them away from the area.

Sometimes on a Late Turn your feet wouldn't hit the ground. You would go from call to call, an audible alarm to domestic, traffic accident to pub fight. On a daily basis it could be that varied. Conversely it could be dead. Take a Sunday Late shift. This was in the days when the licencing laws only allowed for a couple of drinking hours at lunchtime and pubs were shut on a Sunday evening. Pretty much all the shops and supermarkets were closed. There might be the odd corner shop and a few petrol stations, but this was before they had become mini markets and, in many instances, these would be closed too.

This incident is another true story, published many years ago in Police Review Magazine in the 'Dogberry Faux Pas' section. Dogberry is a character from the Shakespeare play 'Much Ado About Nothing'. He was the leader of a bunch of clumsy and poor watchmen. A colleague and friend thought the following was just the sort of thing they were looking for. Now, many years later, I can tell it myself. Firstly, it's important to put this into context and develop the lead up to the incident as a little bit of mitigation on my part. That being said, it is still funny and I am a buffoon!

I was on a foot patrol on one of these quiet Sunday Late Turns. Nothing much was happening; it was about 4.30pm and I was just returning to the station for a bite to eat. I was walking North up Battersea Bridge Road, past some of the low-level blocks of the Surrey Lane Estate. As I looked to my left I caught the briefest of glimpses of a male leaning through the window of one of the flats pointing what appeared to be a crossbow at me. As I dived for cover behind a low brick wall I called for urgent assistance.

Now in my defence, as the entire Relief were swarming out of the canteen in a rush to get to me, I recalled recent incidents of crossbows being brandished on neighbouring grounds, such as Carter Street and Clapham. I had this in my mind as I dropped for cover. It should also be noted that I had not yet realised that I needed spectacles for my impaired vision, something that came into focus shortly afterwards.

It didn't take my colleagues any time at all to reach me. Several had worked out which building I had spotted the crossbow in and had gone there. I was able to point out the window and seconds later a door was put in and after a brief radio silence an 'Old Sweat' cancelled all further units. It transpired that there was a male on scene at the address I had spotted from my concealed position. But he wasn't in possession or aiming any sort of crossbow or other weapon at me.

I am not sure if the incident was resulted over the radio. I like to think not and the Relief spared my blushes, then only for that wonderful friend and colleague to publish it subsequently. In my briefest of glimpses, with my slightly impaired eyesight, what I had actually seen was a SKY engineer leaning through the window offering up the satellite dish bracket he was fitting for the installation of a dish. Oops! I think the front door was repairable and the engineer didn't have any serious injuries!

When I began learning to drive a few weeks later it was discovered (if I didn't know already) that I would need spectacles. I have worn glasses or contact lenses ever since.

There were always shouts of "chasing suspect" over the radio and everyone would go hurtling towards the last known location of the caller. You could hear the heavy breathing and panting as the officer attempted to give a commentary and chase the suspect. On occasion they would be caught but more often than not they would disappear into one of the 'rabbit warren' estates and be lost.

It happened to me from time to time. One such instance, I was operating on one of the patrol cars on a quiet Late Turn before it got dark. My driver that day was a wonderful character, with a huge sense of humour and still now a really good friend. As he drove our Mini Metro Panda car along Broomwood Road towards Clapham Common we spotted something. A youth burst from a small corner shop and ran off towards the common. A man came out of the shop shouting. He told us this young lad had stolen some videos tapes from a rack. I leapt from the car giving chase. My driver got out and did the same. (Unbeknown to me at the time he slipped on his quarter tips and this slowed him down considerably).

I announced on the radio I was chasing a suspect towards The Avenue, which runs across Clapham Common. As my prey ran out into the road he was hit by a car, thrown up into the air and bounced against the windscreen, smashing it, then rolled off the bonnet and on to the tarmac. Dead! Or so I thought.

But, no! Suddenly he's up and off again, continuing across the common towards the bandstand. Even being hit by a moving vehicle at speed didn't seem to slow him. I was 22 years old, played regular sport, my knees were still undamaged by life and I was struggling to catch him. I could hear my colleague shouting, "Go on Guy, get him" and slowly I began to catch up. Clearly the car had impaired his ability to run really fast, so at his new pace I was able to gradually close the gap and with a final effort, I didn't so much as catch him as fall against him and we both ended up on the ground. My driver arrived with a wry smile on his face. He wasn't sure if I'd caught him or just fallen on him either.

This particular colleague was such a character. His humour was infectious and when he moved on to other things, it was a sad loss to the Relief. He was incredibly quick witted and had the right word for everything. This next story is one great example. About a year or so after my arrival on the Relief we got a new Inspector. His predecessor had been content to allow the Sergeants to run things and most of the time left us to our own devices. Our new boss wasn't like this! He wanted to be up to speed on every call, to be apprised of how ongoing matters were progressing. This quickly began to wear. We almost got to the stage when demands for a situation report ("Sit rep, over!") were being asked before we had arrived on scene. He would also try and get to the scene himself. It sometimes felt that he didn't trust us to do the job at all. Maybe he didn't?

My colleague was driving the Area Car (Whisky One) and they took a call to a man on Wandsworth Common carrying and juggling what appeared to the informant, to be a hand grenade. These were different times. The IRA were still very active in London, so it could not be taken as a 'L.O.B'. The Area Car kept up a running commentary of where they were in relation to the Common and other units shouted up that they were heading that way. All the time we could hear, "Situation report please, over," from our new Duty Officer, who was also making his way to the scene.

After several minutes my slightly breathless colleague got on his personal radio and cancelled all further units to the scene. The suspect had been detained and everything was good. What happened was that the Area Car officers had spotted a likely suspect. They had mounted the pavement and driven across one of the football pitches marked out on Wandsworth Common at speed towards the suspect. As they got close to him they could see he was holding a hand grenade. They both, incredibly bravely, got out and wrestled the individual to the ground and relieved him of the article. As they both sat on the suspect catching their respective breaths the Duty Officer appeared. First words out of his mouth?

"Where's your hat, officer"? I kid you not.

To my colleague and friend's eternal salutation he got to his feet and quick as a flash, threw the offending hand grenade at the Duty Officer and said, "Well hold this then!".

He then marched off in the direction of Whisky One to retrieve his hat from the back seat.

I would have paid money to see the Duty Officer's reaction.

The hand grenade was a cunningly fashioned cigarette lighter, by the way! Yes, hilarious!

Probationer Constables had to show a record of work to their reporting Sergeants. It was important to show that you were doing something. One of the main ways to do this was to arrest people and to report them for motoring offences. It had to be something quantifiable and this was in stark contrast to my more experienced colleagues. Take the van driver, with a knack for sniffing out a villain. In his eyes if a motorist committed an offence in front of him he might stop them and have a word. If the motorist was able to understand his transgression, everything else was correct and they passed the 'attitude test', then a suitably polite verbal warning would be given. The reason was that the vast majority of the public never have any contact with the police and when they do, it is most likely for a motoring offence. They would probably have led a trouble-free life and were supportive of the police. Why make them change their thoughts about the law? Providing no harm had been done, then discretion would have the desired effect.

As well as 'Chasing Suspects' going out over the radio, the other guaranteed way of clearing the canteen and getting everyone running was a cry for urgent assistance. One of these might be an officer struggling on his own with a prisoner or being overwhelmed at a disturbance. It was never taken lightly and no one ever cried wolf. If you called for urgent assistance, that was exactly what you got; every time.

A fight at The Butchers Arms was not uncommon. Mainly frequented by residents of the Patmore Estate it was on the extremity of our ground and a bugger to get to. Situated in Thessaly Road at the junction with Ascalon Street, all vehicle access was via the Wandsworth Road. With hindsight, I always wondered why the Patmore Estate wasn't policed by Clapham, their station was in Union Grove, just across the road. Or, it would also have been easier if the two arterial roads of the Patmore had joined with Nine Elms Lane, instead of ending just short. Unless you had a Fireman's drop key (never), you had to go all the way up Queenstown Road, along the Wandsworth Road and then into the estate by either Stewarts Road or Thessaly Road. Knowing this when a cry went up on the Patmore we always went mob handed.

When you got a shout like this, a good distance from the station, it was often the case the disturbance, fight, altercation, call it what you will, would be over, done and dusted before you even got close. If it was on licensed premises, the Landlord would have got a grip on things and there would be no need to involve the police. As a convoy of fast-moving police motor vehicles, you would get a cancellation over the radio and could return to the canteen to finish your grub.

On this occasion, the cancellation never came and the officer on scene was detailing the ongoing, full blown "ding-dong". We had been able to scrape together about 15 officers in three vehicles, mainly crammed in the back of the van. The driver of the van was double de- clutching and revving the engine as we squealed and drifted around corners and flew down the Wandsworth Road.

Sure enough, on arrival, it was still rocking! A bar stool crashed through one of the windows as we were getting out of the van. It was like something out of the Wild West. The Section Sergeant's plan, after securing the safety of the officer on the scene, was to bring the melée to a quick conclusion. Enter the premises en masse and try to stop the fighting. His belief was that some of the patrons will flee and those that hang around? Well, let's see how that goes first. So, in we charged.

It was a proper fight. Glasses, bottles and furniture were being thrown. People punching and kicking each other and arming themselves with pool cues and Toby Jugs. We just charged in and started fighting too. A few more left the bar and the remaining half dozen or so were quickly subdued and we sat them on the floor. Six arrests were made. All charged with one or another public order offence. No other allegations were made. The Landlord was keen to sort it out himself and we knew the majority of those involved. Chances are they'd be at it again the following weekend. None of us had been injured (well not seriously) and the disturbance had been dealt with. The Sergeant wrote a report for the Licensing Officer and we all had an arrest for our record of work books, but that was about it.

The Butchers or Battersea Arms, as it was subsequently called, is closed now. Just a small derelict building surrounded by a selection of new blocks. But it did have a history. When we all burst in there to quell that disturbance it would have been 1987 or 88.

Some years before that, it had been the haunt of luminaries such as members of rock bands 'The Who' and 'Thin Lizzy'. The Who had a recording studio just around the corner in Thessaly Road, where they recorded the album Quadrophenia.

You learnt a good deal about each other in these situations. This was long before Officer Safety courses were introduced. It was a fight and you just got involved. I got punched in the face and had objects thrown at me. Getting punched in the face is quite shocking to most people. While at Hendon, we had to undertake a round of 'milling', which is where you are paired in weight with someone, issued boxing gloves, head guards and gum shields and told to punch each other continuously for one minute. I always presumed to get you used to just this sort of experience. To have it happen on a regular basis as part of your job though, is a little different. As a profession it sets you apart and maybe in recent times, the public and powers that be, have lost sight of that. It was a fight. People got hurt, we got hurt. You became part of the team. You could be relied upon in a ruck. You learned never to fight fair, always have superior numbers and made sure your notes detailed as much as you could recall.

Beat Duty (Night Shift)

Packed lunch placed in the D Relief fridge.
There is no canteen, self-sufficient on Nights.
Parade and a briefing. Postings, vehicles and beats to allocate.
A mug of tea with banter, before donning raincoats and gloves. Rain is light.

Foot patrolling in pairs. A neighbour dispute, one for the Council.
On to the Surrey Lane Estate, all towers and linked walkways.
Heading to a domestic, we squeeze past a drunk being ill.
Eighth floor venue; wife is by the lift. "He's inside", she says.

"Police! We're coming in". Down the hall, sticks drawn.
Place is a tip. Suspect in the lounge swaying in his pants.
Came quietly after a slap and a kick; raincoat torn.
Cuffed in the lift. His face against the wall, covered in spit.

One in the bin, wife in a refuge, Custody Sergeant happy.
Writing my notes coincides with a bag of chips.
A report of afters at the Prince Albert; patrons ejected, make it snappy.
Back in for refs. Check the duty boards upstairs, but keep it quiet while CID kips.

Get to crew Whisky One after refs; operator at court in the morning.
Urgent assistance over the river; operating the mains set to overcome.
Cancelled prior, sufficient units attending.
Back in at Six. Tried to be home before the rush hour began.

I liked Night Duty. Once you got used to the unnatural lack of sleep and the inability to rest during the day it was a great shift to work. You had the station to yourself. No senior management or civvies floating about. Once you cleared the Late Turn's back log of calls and the pubs had all shut at 11pm, you had the rest of the night to go out and patrol and actually catch people doing stuff! It was brilliant.

As a young officer I would spend the first few years of Night Duty on foot. It was possible to double up on a vehicle after refs, but that was all down to the benevolence of the Section Sergeant and the weather. Foot Duty officers would patrol in pairs and in those days, we had sufficient numbers to double man the vehicles and still put out four or five pairs of 'walkers'.

We patrolled the back streets and the estates, advising youths to get themselves home and following some to ensure they did. Maybe society was different then. When we asked people to disperse, on the whole they did. Those that didn't got a rigorous search and maybe a night in the cells. It was my patch and after a few months I knew most of the main players by name. I knew everything about my ground. When I started, I was given a map of Wandsworth Borough and told to learn it. Learn it, I did. I would walk down the small narrow cut throughs and alleyways, knowing where these short cuts would take me. If someone, for example, talked about the North West Frontier estate, off Falcon Road, I knew where Cabul, Candahar, Khyber and Afghan Roads were.

While writing this story, I was curious as to why such names were used. I discovered it was simply because the houses were planned, designed and built at the time of both the Second Anglo-Afghan war (1878-1880) and the Anglo-Zulu war (1879). Rowena Crescent was originally called Zulu Crescent. The whole area was officially known as Falcon Park. Some street names that no longer exist from that area include Kambala, Musjid, Natal and Tugela Roads.

I would patrol over the footbridges and along the estate's aerial walkways. I would know which pubs had the after-hours 'lock- ins' and which restaurants would be happy to serve me a cup of tea in their kitchens before closing time.

There was an old adage that a good police officer never got wet. As a police officer walking the beat in the depths of winter, there was every chance I could get wet. But with passed on knowledge, I very quickly found places to shelter from the elements. I remember an 'Old Sweat' telling me how he could get a bag of chips and a pint of beer under his then service issue cape and no one would know. By the time I joined, capes were gone, replaced by the previously mentioned, useless raincoat. No amount of chips could be secreted inside there. But on occasion I could be found in the kitchen of a very supportive restaurant having a plate of something, washed down with a suitably refreshing beverage. Safe to say there were places to find shelter. You just needed to know where.

After parade there was time for a brew before starting patrols. The Section Sergeant would sometimes send us out if we were spending too long gossiping. That first couple of hours could be busy. Some calls the Late Turn hadn't been able to deal with and perhaps the odd bit of noise or disturbance as the pubs turned out their patrons. Another frequent call out was for some sort of domestic dispute. These could take on a variety of forms and they didn't always happen on Nights, but most did. In my experience, the perpetrator was always the husband or boyfriend and the victim(s) was invariably the wife, girlfriend and kids. Alcohol or drugs seemed to be the catalyst to get things going, before a neighbour, relative or even the victim themselves would call us.

When you went to one of these, you never knew what you were going to get. Sometimes the assailant would have said his piece, made his point with his fists and then run out of puff and be asleep on the settee. On other rare occasions the victim would have fought back and the assailant would be injured. One such call, a lady let us in to show us her husband unconscious on the floor, surrounded by several pieces of a broken flowerpot under the ironing board. Closer examination revealed he wasn't breathing and didn't have a pulse. Some basic first aid was administered while we waited for an ambulance and detained the woman, as a precaution. She explained there had been an almighty argument and her husband had shoved her. She had reached out and grabbed the first thing that came to hand, a flowerpot, and hit her husband over the head with it. He collapsed. Not from the effects of the flowerpot, but, as we later discovered, he had a major heart attack as they were arguing and was dead before he crashed to the floor next to the ironing board. She was initially arrested for murder, which was quickly dropped, when the circumstances became clear.

Another Night Duty call out was to a woman who was waiting for us by the lift when we got to the 8 or 9th floor of the block where she lived on the Surrey Lane Estate, just behind the station. She looked pretty beaten up and in need of treatment for her visible injuries. We could hear her husband shouting the odds from inside the flat. I didn't ask any questions at that time, it was obvious the lady had been badly assaulted and the person responsible was in the flat. My colleague radioed for an ambulance and some back up, that would need to include the van.

We decided to enter, both of us had our sticks drawn. The noise was coming from the living room. There, in all his glory was a slightly overweight, white male in his late thirties swaying in just his underpants in front of the television. He must have caught a glimpse of us out of the corner of his eye or our reflection in the television because he turned and lurched towards us. I think he was telling us to get the fuck out of his house, but it came out as an incoherent spittle-flecked roar. He managed to grab the front of my raincoat, immediately ripping two buttons off. I couldn't use my stick, he was too close, so I punched him in the face and as he fell back, my colleague and I jumped on him. Somehow in the mass of bodies we got him on his front and after a few more punches / elbows were thrown, we got the handcuffs on and lifted him to his feet. That's when he started spitting at us in earnest. He was thrown face first against the nearest wall, while we radioed for just the van, cancelling all other units.

I hate spitting. It's just not nice. You see footballers on the television doing it and it just looks horrible. The pitch must be covered in it by the end of a game. Anyway, quite a few prisoners would spit once they were handcuffed, so you quickly learned to face them away from you, in the days before spit hoods. On the subject of handcuffing. When Officer Safety came along in the 1990's there were rules of when to and not to handcuff. Really!? I always worked on the basis that the person being cuffed was either a high or an unknown threat. I would therefore handcuff everyone, with hands to the rear and then conduct a proper search. Keep it simple. If you get arrested you will be handcuffed, with your hands to the rear. No exceptions. Just tell the public that's what will happen. They will soon get it.

Back to our domestic spitter. We got him into the lift, where he continued to decorate the lift walls with his phlegm. He was thrown in the back of the van, face down on the footwell and my colleague and I sat on the bench seats opposite each other with our feet on him. The Section Sergeant and the ambulance had turned up and went upstairs to talk to the injured wife to see what she wanted to do about this latest fracas. Back then, to get any sort of prosecution you needed a victim statement. But the victims were loath to give one. He's their husband. He had a temper, but he was a diamond really. Can you just keep him in until the morning? He'll be good as gold by then. Eventually after repeated beatings some of the victims did prosecute. We might go for a breach of the peace and lengthy reports to Social Services, especially if kids were involved. First aid and trips to the hospital with the victims were common.

Every Relief had a blagger. Someone who could 'obtain' things. Not at the level of the afore mentioned Property Officer, but you get the idea. We had our own 'King Mumper' on the Relief. He always got a hard time, but most of it, like everything on the Relief, was light-hearted banter and everyone benefitted from his procurements. After the initial flurry of calls died down around midnight we would all return to the station for a brew. This coincided nicely with our Chief Blagger delivering a huge bag of chips he had purloined from the local 'Chippy' just as they were closing. There was more than enough for everyone to have a handful to go with their tea.

Calls to pubs serving customers after hours were fairly common. Most of the time this practice went unnoticed. It only came to light if the noise rose above a certain level and a neighbour or passers-by complained. Then we had to at least make our presence known and either close it down or result it as a private party. This was usually because it was where the CID were drinking that particular month.

Refs were taken at about 2am. Some brought sandwiches from home. Others would occasionally cook something themselves on the cooker located next to all the Relief food lockers. We went through a stage of frequenting a Kebab shop in the parade near to Clapham South tube station. The proprietor had developed a Kebab Roll. A long sausage shaped piece of cooked spiced lamb with onions all wrapped tightly in a flat bread. But it was the sauce drizzled through that made it. A fiery red sauce that would make you catch your breath. Then a green sauce, that was just a motherfucker! Green sauce please!

Once I had settled into Relief life, I let it be known that I had worked in a restaurant before starting as a cop. Not haute cuisine, but I knew my way around a kitchen. My Section Sergeant seized upon this and the next month on Nights I was cooking the Relief a meal on the small four ringed cooker in the canteen. The first time was a huge chilli with rice and bread. It became a bit of a regular occurrence to cook a meal once during the week. I even progressed to having access to the proper canteen kitchen. The one I recall most; was the time I was busy preparing a Lasagne. It was a windy night in October. Windy? I should say so! While cooking, I could hear my colleagues over the radio describing trees collapsing across Clapham Common and crashing through people's houses. At one stage all the lights went out across the Borough. We had a backup generator at the station, so we were ok.

This was not just your average storm and despite what Michael Fish said, it has gone down in history as the great Hurricane of 1987. By the time I was ready to serve the troops their Lasagne, we had a canteen full of refugees from their destroyed houses. After discussion with the Duty Officer and working out what quantity of food I had prepared, we decided to offer our enforced 'guests' some food, while they struggled to come to terms with their situation. I wonder what they thought? Turfed out of bed in the middle of the night when a tree crashes through your house and having to take refuge in the local police station in pyjamas. After a cup of tea had been provided, suddenly an officer appears in an apron offering freshly cooked Lasagne. They must have thought they were dreaming.

The station was very quiet on Nights. When you were in having refs, you could wander about and have a look in people's offices, try and find out what was going on. You could go to the Duties Office to see what they had in store for you for the coming month. This was in the days before computers did it all, and the Duties for everyone were on large paper covered wooden boards, written in pencil. You could see if you were allocated a posting on the Area Car or if you'd copped the football at the weekend. You could see if your annual leave request had been approved and written on to the boards. I am sure some of the more seasoned on the Relief were able to adjust their own postings with their own eraser and pencil. It never entered my head, your Worship!

The Area Car was the glamour posting. Back then, it was the only car that was fitted with proper blue lights and the familiar wailing siren everyone recognises today. Other cars had a blue revolving light, but no noise. The van was fitted with a switch, that if you held it down a bell would sound. That was just embarrassing! The Area Car was an SD1 Rover with a two and a half litre engine. It went like crazy, but had crap brakes and the turning circle of a small super tanker. If it was broken, you would get a spare traffic car, which would be the 3.5 litre V8 Rover. Far too fast for Battersea, but immense fun! The drivers were all 'Old Sweats'. Advanced Drivers you see. A six-week course to be able to push these cars about. There was always talk of a particular table in the canteen being for Advanced Drivers only. I don't recall such a thing on D Relief, but I did hold our Area Car Drivers in high esteem.

My first taste of operating on the Area Car was the last half of Nights from 2am until we finished. The posted operator was at Court the following morning, so he had gone home early. My driver was a quiet chap. He had a habit of coughing a couple of times to clear his throat and then he would sniff. He smoked the thinnest roll up cigarettes I have ever seen, perhaps one or two strands of tobacco at most and he could roll them with one hand. He may not have realised it was my first time sitting in an Area Car, but he made me feel comfortable. He showed me how and then got me to do a signal check on the Mains set radio. That's the one that links to Scotland Yard, rather than the Battersea divisional radios we all carried. The Area Car and one or two CID cars were the only vehicles fitted with these. He took time to explain the mains set radio procedure and generally aid my knowledge and ease my nerves. On his nod we took a call for assistance over the water (The River Thames) in the Kings Road, Chelsea. The Area Car had a remit to roam beyond the divisional boundaries. We were cancelled prior to arrival, but it was my first ever shout in the Area Car and that's when I decided that I wanted to be an Advanced Driver on the Relief.

The last couple of hours of Nights could be hard. Through some of my early years I walked a foot patrol for the whole eight hours. That could be challenging. You tried everywhere to find a villain up to no good, so you could bring a 'body' into custody and the warm, dry station. Sometimes we had sufficient troops on duty to post a plain clothed observer in the back of the Area Car. Then he or she could be dropped off in a likely spot, to see if they could witness some nefarious activity. An officer might get up on the roof of an appropriate block with a pair of decent binoculars and scope the roads carefully, witness a motor vehicle thief at it and radio the location to the rest of us, so we could pounce! Catching wrongun's in the act! Sounds almost unheard of today.

Failing that, a colleague in a vehicle might take pity on you and pick you up. The van was a common one for that. When you were posted to a vehicle and it got to 4-4.30am, most of the time you were performing a 'listening watch' while you rested your eyes, parked up in a variety of discreet spots on the ground. This was fine as a pair. The idea being at least one of you would wake up in time to get back to the station before being dismissed. Posted on your own and parking up to 'rest your eyes' was sometimes dangerous. We once waited at the top of the stairs at the back of the Nick to be dismissed, waiting for one of the patrol cars to return. It eventually went on long enough for us to have to go out and look for our missing colleague. Luckily, one of the other drivers knew his favourite park up spot and found him sound asleep. That cost him a few bacon sandwiches.

Battersea Police also had the stray dogs list to deal with towards the end of the Night shift. All the dogs that had been found or handed in were listed by each police station in the Met. and this complete list was printed out at our station, for someone to run it down to the world-famous Battersea Dog's Home, so they could go out and collect all the dogs around London that morning. Most nights there was a sweepstake to see if you could correctly guess the total number of dogs on the list.

The last thing you want on Nights is to be late off. You come back into the station for 5.30am ready to be dismissed and on your way home as early as possible. I suppose I was fortunate to live so close back then and I could race back to the section house on my motorbike and be in bed before 6.30am. If I could get to sleep before the world around me started moving about and preparing itself for the day then personally speaking, I could sleep until about 1 or 2 in the afternoon. This would then give me a few hours to do stuff while the shops and banks etc were still open. I could get a decent hot meal from the Section House canteen and then chill before leaving for work again around 9.15pm.

Nights were great. I remember them fondly but they certainly wear you down. I did Night Duty for the first 16 years of my service and then found a role that didn't include them. I remember being so tired on duty, struggling to keep my eyes open. It was always easier when we were busy, you just kept going. Some of my colleagues thrived on it and did some of the best proactive police work in those difficult hours between about 3.30 and 5.30am.

My friend, the young van driver, as well as a sixth sense for villainy was also lucky. On one particular night we were both posted on the van and driving slowly around the ground, heading to one of his favourite spots to park up and grab a quick kip. We were heading down Lavender Hill. We had gone past the Battersea Arts Centre, past Nancy Lams restaurant and were crawling along down the hill to the lights with Queenstown Road and Cedars Road. The lights changed just as we got there and we turned left into Queenstown Road. Just around the corner on the left was a small Off License / Newsagents. There was this shabby old BMW parked outside with its boot open. Suddenly a male comes out of the shop carrying a slab of drink, sees us, drops the crate and is away running on foot.

Quick as a flash my oppo puts up that we have 'suspects on' and gives the location. I was out and chasing the male who'd dropped the crate. I think my driver was doing the same, having found another person to chase. It's hard to recall when you're chasing a villain, trying to radio where you are, check on your mucker and clamber over brick walls covered in no climb paint, all at the same time.

"902, location, over"

"He's just in front of me, I'm in the gardens of the flats at the back of the shops that are up on Lavender Hill, near Queenstown Road, over", I had no clue where I was or what the flats were called.

"He's near Ashley Crescent, over", someone knew roughly where I was.

"Suspect detained, I'm near a metal fence by a low block of flats, no road name, over". I'd caught the bloke, who thankfully just gave it up the moment I jumped on him, so I was able to cuff him and catch my breath.

"Yeah, that's one of the blocks in Ashley Crescent, I'll go to 902, other units go to the scene, Whisky One, over.

I sat on my prisoner and waited for my colleagues to arrive and listened as the rest of my Relief swarmed up to the scene.

We had detained two of a three handed burglary team. My man was a known associate of the person shown as the registered keeper of the abandoned BMW outside the off licence. He was the outstanding suspect. The car was registered to an address just around the corner, so a very quick drive to that location gave us the third suspect and the main player of the team. In addition to the burglary, a substantial quantity of stolen property was discovered at the third suspects address and a nice big bag full of amphetamine in the boot of the Beemer.

I remember it more for the way the Relief all got involved to assist in the investigation in some way. An exhibits officer appointed himself, someone securing the scene, others taking witness and victim statements. Everyone had a walk on part. It was even enough of a job to wake the Night Duty CID up. It was one of those great jobs where six months later we all headed down to Kingston Crown Court for a day out to give our evidence, as they'd all pleaded Not Guilty. I think for most of us it was a rest day without notice too! A cracking evening of drinking ending up in a curry house. As for the villains. They were all found guilty.

Robbery

Theft using force. They call it a robbery.
Flash a blade and demand the bag.
Like magpies attracted to anything shiny.
They rip away jewellery and watches. That's their usual swag.

The victims tend to be young women.
But any who are vulnerable, on quiet streets are prey.
Followed from the bus or the train.
A punch or other threat. "Give me your bag!" is what they say.

Casual and frequent. The perpetrators are blatant.
The victims are left violated, traumatised and shaken.
Descriptions and profiles are hastily circulated.
Covert surveillance at The Junction is undertaken.

Suspects are black, white or asian.
Stopped and searched. Arrested, charged and bailed.
Oh! And one hapless goon in a turban!
A conveyor belt of violent criminals, who are seldom jailed.

Crime prevention advice both sought and given.
Women's self-defence courses put in place.
Recidivists arrested and then to court they are driven.
But Magistrates Courts dither. "We just don't have the space".

During my first few years of service the Borough was suffering from a huge amount of robbery, perpetrated by a very small number of young suspects. The majority of whom were black males aged between about 14 and 17 years. I don't describe this as some sort of sweeping racial thing, it was just a statistical fact at that moment in time on our small Battersea Division the majority of the robbers were black. The only important thing about skin colour to me was that it helped in trying to find these robbers. When a victim describes his or her assailant one of the most important descriptive factors is whether they are black, white, Dark European, Asian, Arabic or Oriental looking. From there you can go on to list, build, height, clothing and any noticeable distinguishing features beyond that. You would be surprised how many robbers always wore the same coat, jacket or baseball cap when they were up to no good.

It felt like a conveyor belt of crime. Robbers would be identified and caught. They would be charged and a case would be prepared for Court. Sometimes we would give these 'scrotes' bail from the police station, sometimes we'd let the Courts do it. It was highly likely they would commit many more crimes whilst on bail and before the Courts realised it they were handing out justice for a dozen or so similar offences of robbery, burglary, criminal damage etc.

It was incredibly rare for a custodial sentence to be given, so you'd just wait for them to commit their next crime and catch them. It never felt like we dealt with it; more like we just kicked it down the road.

I don't know why some choose to rob people. I don't have a profiling degree to be able to assess the 'wronguns'. From my perspective, these robbers were just a bad lot who needed dealing with. They traumatised victims, often changing their lives. I could never see an excuse for it. We tried many ways to lower the sheer number of robberies. Tried to help victims to be more careful, suggest they remove jewellery and watches from obvious display. Where possible, walk home down busier, well-lit streets. Use an authorised taxi to take them to their doors. Have their keys ready in hand as they approach their front door. We even set up and ran a Women's Self-Defence course. This provided detailed advice and some basic self-defence training to assist the vulnerable and anyone who we felt would benefit from this.

Then we tried to square up the suspects. Plenty of stop and searches of the known players on the ground. Make them know they are being watched the whole time. It's their choice really. They didn't have to rob people. Most of the stops would yield a knife or some stolen gear, so add another charge to the list of cases the Juvenile Court wouldn't deal with.

There were occasions when a suspect might be picked up. Usually after dark and driven some distance off the ground and just dumped there. It seems simplistic now, but it felt like we were just giving the general public in Battersea a bit of a breather until this wanker found his way home. I don't know whether this was the case when one of our most prolific robbers had been gone for a while and we received a call from a constabulary station. It transpired that he'd wound up in Halifax! (Good effort that!) and there had been a massive spike in their robbery figures almost overnight. They'd caught our young man and had him in custody. They pleaded with us to take him back to London. Someone off the Relief drove up to Halifax and brought him back to Battersea on a Night Duty.

This was the same chap who nearly escaped from custody at Battersea. He was an incredibly thin wiry little fucker. He somehow got through the wicket in the cell door (we believe this to be the case as nobody admitted leaving the cell door open). The wicket is the small metal flap that opens in the cell door, usually to allow food and other items to be passed to the prisoner, without the need to open the door. The Custody Suite had a two door 'airlock' system, with two keypad numbers needed to unlock each door and let you out into the rest of the station and towards the Front Office. He was able to get through the first door and was caught when the gaoler returned from the canteen, ironically with a tray of prisoner's meals to be confronted by the skinny little robber stuck in-between the doors in the 'airlock'. The gaoler saw the amusement in the situation and asked the lad to open the charge room door and walked him back inside.

Robbers would often run as a gang. If you identified one, you would know who all the other suspects were! Part of me wondered if it was stupidity on their part. More realistically it was probably arrogance that even when they were caught, nothing would happen to them. On the rare occasion that the Courts did finally pass a reasonable sentence, the majority were juveniles, so they were indoctrinated into the Feltham Young Offenders juvenile crime school and returned to us ten times worse.

One gang we were dealing with were probably stupid rather than arrogant; well at least one of their number was really stupid……

….."Listen I appreciate it's difficult and it was dark and it all happened very quickly, but is there anything you can recall about them that we can use to try and find them"?

"Well, it did happen very quickly. It was all a bit of a blur as they ripped my handbag off my shoulder. There must have been five or six of them, all probably teenagers. Their clothing was dark and some of them had white trainers on, but I remember one of them was wearing a turban!"

Bingo! "Thanks love, yep that will do nicely".

It was just too easy. We had loads of villains all neatly card indexed in the Collators Office (computers were still several years away). Plenty of robbery cards of all ethnicities, ages and genders. But as far as I can recall, just the one lad in the card index system who wore a turban. A lone Sikh 'wrongun' on the manor!

It was then just a drive to his known address and another day of shame for his family as we once more carted him off to the Nick. The despair on his mum's face was palpable. They were a hard-working, decent Sikh family and their son was just a feral monster, completely out of control. Years later I do wonder if he decided that this was the best way for him, living in an Inner London suburb to blend in, avoid being bullied, racially abused or even being a victim himself.

Notting Hill

Sold as a weekend Carnival of community fun.
An annual two-day headache to try and avoid.
The traditional Sunday children's parade in the sun.
By the end of Monday all hospitality and fun, devoid.

When young in service it was an annual leave cancelling must.
The saving grace was the provision of double time on Monday.
Fed and briefed on tiny school chairs, then into the melee thrust.
Get to a cordon, work as a group. On ground assigned stay.

I never danced, blew a whistle or lent out my helmet.
My role was to be discreet and act professionally.
Helpful, polite and resilient, but stoic features set.
An early Sunday finish, gone in daylight. No need to dally.

Monday, bussed in earlier to our Sir Isaac Newton school base.
A longer briefing as trouble expected when the sound systems end.
The mood changes on the ground as steaming teams chase.
Told to hold our position. "More troops needed, please send".

Missiles launched at us as darkness falls.
No body armour or shields. Just a tunic and helmet with straps fitted.
"Ok, stay as a group, just keep together", our experienced skipper calls.
Another Carnival ends once more with us inappropriately kitted!

When you were young in service there was no way you could get out of policing Notting Hill. Maybe once you had your feet under the table a little bit you could negotiate with the Duties Office and possibly be given an alternative. But for about the first five to six years of my service, every August for two days I had to put up with the Notting Hill Carnival.

It was just dreadful. Loads of people determined to have a good time on the tiny streets of a London Borough. A chance to blow whistles, openly smoke cannabis and build great totemic speaker stacks and blast shit music out into the night. I hated everything about the Carnival. It was without question the most awful two tours of duty of the year.

You were always posted for the two days. Sometimes looking ahead on the Duties Boards, you would see that you were supposed to be Night Duty that week and thought that might be enough to get you out of it. Not a chance. They put you on Lates on the Saturday, then you were available for Sunday and Monday's fun! I remember you couldn't take annual leave as a single day or two days. The leave had to be part of a proper two-week holiday and even then, it was very limited numbers who managed to get the time off.

Sunday morning at some ridiculous time, you would parade at Battersea in long sleeved shirts and ties, tunics and raincoats were carried. The decision about shirt sleeve order could be taken by the Gold Commander once you were there and the thing got going. Get on the coach and smile at the rows of familiar faces from the rest of W District, who once again had been dragged in to police the bloody Carnival.

It may not have always been, but I have an idea that our briefing and ref's area was at The Sir Isaac Newton School for boys in Lancaster Road, not far from Ladbroke Grove. It was a primary school for kids up to age eleven, so the chairs, tables and toilets were built for them, not for several hundred oversized fat-arsed cops. We would get fed a hot meal. I think in my first couple of years this happened at the school. For a few years after that, until I could finally wheedle my way out of doing the thing, we were fed at Buckingham Gate and then bussed over to The Alamo (sorry, Notting Hill).

There was a briefing, which to be fair I listened to in my first year. Be vigilant, use discretion. Don't arrest for minor infractions of the law and watch each other's backs. Let the thing happen and be courteous and respectful. Make sure everyone is ground assigned when the sound systems have to be turned off; that's usually the kicker that sends the thing into orbit.

Sergeants; make sure you are on the correct radio channel. That was always amusing on aid in those days. You didn't each get a radio. I can only presume because there weren't enough to go around. Each serial of about ten officers led by a Sergeant would be given a street or a junction to take up position on. There would be a load of great big heavy cordon railings ominously stacked high for deployment should, well when, it became necessary to close the street and stop people from going down it.

We would get some downtime in the school after the briefing. Because we had paraded so ridiculously early, we usually had a couple of hours to kill before we needed to be ground assigned. A card school would start up. The smokers would go out into the playground or behind the bike sheds for a smoke. There were usually some newspapers to read and a video recorder with a very limited selection of films to watch.

Sunday was the Children's parade in the morning. Always seemed to go off without a hitch and then there would be a lull in the afternoon as people set up their food stalls and got the previously mentioned stereo systems plugged in. I think in those first few years the early starting serials like us on W got dismissed at a reasonable time. On occasion it may well have been even before it got dark.

Sunday was also usually the day when the media would get their money shot of an officer dancing and cavorting with the street revellers. The classic shot of someone other than the officer wearing his Beat Duty helmet, while he blew a whistle for all he was worth. Not my idea of fun! I was there to police, act in a professional manner and be a uniformed presence on the streets. I was not, in my opinion, there to join in.

By the time I got back to the Section House, that first year, it was 10pm. Oh! Still time for a couple of pints of 'Hooligan' at The Court Tavern then.

Another stupidly early parade on the Monday morning, but that was ok. It was a Bank Holiday, double time. The 'Old Sweats', furious to have once again been caught up in this shit, were determined they would milk the thing for all it was worth.

One year we were paraded later in the day, knowing that meant we were definitely there for the duration, but on this occasion, I recall we thought we would be dismissed late afternoon, perhaps early evening at the latest. That would have realised about 12 hours at double time and avoid the majority of grief that a Monday at Notting Hill tended to bring.

On this particular year there was plenty of grub once we got to the school base. Then we were out on a foot patrol in pairs. Walking the streets of Notting Hill, about twenty to thirty officers walking down to All Saints Road and then doing three left turns before walking down All Saints Road again.

They had been doing these highly visible foot patrols around the immediate area surrounding All Saints Road some months before the Carnival in August. You would get fed at Buckingham Gate, then bussed down to Notting Hill to perform these pointless patrols. One radio between two! At any time, it was possible to see the pair in front and the pair behind as we walked along. I never really got the idea of what we were supposed to be doing? Ease tensions between the community and the police? Remind the locals that we had a lot of officers available? Thankfully, these extraordinary patrols only happened to me once!

After a couple of hours of walking these streets, watching the skyscraper sound towers get erected on virtually every street corner, we were relieved and headed back to our school base for a cup of tea and some snacks. Another briefing was delivered to advise us that intelligence has suggested that there could be trouble this evening with 'steaming' gangs expected to run amok through the masses of people gathered. Steaming is when a large gang would charge through a crowd ripping jewellery, watches and stealing other property as they ran. Victims would also discover that they might have been slashed with a craft or carpet knife as the gang ran past.

I was aware that we had plain clothes officers out on the streets trying to identify these 'steaming' teams. But with a gang of over twenty, all they could do was spot and hope that a couple of District Support Units (DSU's) were close by who might be able to stop at least some of them. This was before the formation of the Territorial Support Group (TSG). The police love a change of title. The DSU itself was the successor to the famous Special Patrol Group (SPG). Keep changing the letters, keep the public guessing.

As the afternoon wore on and we did another aimless patrol of the ever more crowded streets it all started to change, as the Carnival seemingly does every year. It goes from being a fun day of community revelry to a dark and dangerous environment. Too much alcohol and weed, loud bass driven music on a warm summers evening, with different and rival sections of the community coming together. Easy access from the tube stations to attend, leading to mass overcrowding on this tiny collection of streets in West London.

We were back in for another brew and dived into the boxes of snacks to get the better biscuits and crisps. It was probably about 7 or 8pm by now and even insulated inside the school the heavy bass beat of the sound systems pulsed through your head.

Our skipper returned from a mini briefing with the Inspector. We were to form a cordon at the junction of Lancaster Road and Ladbroke Grove.

There were about ten of us plus our skipper and initially we split ourselves into equal numbers on each pavement at that location. When the trouble started, we were to drag the stacked cordon barriers across the road and prevent anyone getting up Lancaster Road towards the school. I loved the fact that we knew trouble was going to happen, it was just a question of when?

We could hear snippets of radio traffic from the Sergeant's radio, clearly it was getting quite tasty in another street not far from us. It's incredibly frustrating to be stood waiting for something to happen, you can hear colleagues on the Sergeants radio having problems, but you have to stay in at your location. All we could do was listen, unstack the barriers and start hooking them together. Trouble was upon us!

We created squares with four barriers then hooked these squares together across the road. It provided a strong barrier and created a distance between us and the mass of humanity on Ladbroke Grove. You could see some people were clearly trying to get out of the area now, caught up in something which was no longer a Carnival. We tried to pull people and families out of the crowd to aid their departure down Lancaster Road.

We heard via the radio that the order had been given to turn the sound systems off early. I reckon this would have been about 8.30pm. Here we go then. This always seemed to be the final element in the gathering tension that would tip things towards outright hostility. Sure enough, within a couple of minutes the first bottle sailed over our heads and smashed in the road behind us.

When things get thrown at you I always wondered what started it? I was aware that a steaming gang had been stopped at the bottom of Ladbroke Grove, near the tube entrance and there was a ruck going on there between DSU's and the gang. But then other people in the crowd were coming to the aid of the gang. These things escalate very quickly. We, unlike the DSU's, were not in flame proof overalls, knee protectors, NATO Helmets with visors down, carrying short shields and long batons. No. We had recently put on our tunics over shirt sleeve order and now had the straps down on our Beat Duty helmets. No body armour, no shields, just every day Beat Duty uniform.

My first couple of Notting Hill's I wasn't Level 2 shield trained anyway. But at least half of the officers with me were and all their protective kit was neatly bagged on the top of their lockers at the Nick, gathering dust. That's why there is so much archive footage of officers carrying dustbin lids and No Waiting cones. You defended yourself with whatever you could grab. Some additional officers had appeared at our position and the order was reinforced that we kept the area behind us in Lancaster Road sterile and clear so other units could be deployed through our cordon when necessary.

We had a bit of a void in front of our position out into Ladbroke Grove. The massed crowds had thinned out. The DSU cadre of officers and their arrested persons came through our cordon, to await transport away from the area. That increased the abundance of missiles heading our way from across the road, the other side of the junction. A couple of colleagues went down, hit by missiles. One lad got hit on the back of the head by half a house brick as he was kneeling to avoid other stuff. I think we all got hit by something that evening. I copped a piece of brick on my arm and was lucky when a bottle smashed on a wall just above my head.

Additional DSU units appeared behind us and gradually moved the missile throwers out of range. During this lull it became clear that elsewhere had been a good deal worse and there had been a fatality amongst the crowd. A member of the public had been stabbed and had bled out at the scene. Serious and heart breaking as this was, it reduced the numbers on the streets drastically and things very quickly died down. Is that what it takes to quell this disorder? Someone had turned up to a family fun day out, to a community coming together to celebrate and been stabbed to death!

Another Carnival over. On the bus on the way back to Battersea we were all quiet. I was knackered. It had been a long two days, it always was. I came away with a few cuts and bruises. The lad who stopped the house brick with his head had a concussion and stitches but was back at work within a few weeks. In all, I think I did about five or six Carnivals. In the years ahead, I did everything I could to avoid it!

Aid at Wapping

The picket line had been corralled back to order.
The paving slab missiles and iron railings are stopping.
As reinforcements, we were bussed in. Sat on a border.
Between print workers and News International, Wapping.

Freezing blasts of icy wind chilled us to the core.
As we were paired up and patrolled down Cable Street.
Teapot One arrived. The chilli beef pie was incredibly poor.
Weather is on the turn. Shit! It's starting to sleet.

Back on the bus at 3am; A card school underway.
Old sweats swinging the lamp with Miner's strike stories.
I grab some shut eye on overtime pay.
One ear listening to tall tales of past glories.

Jolted awake as Bronze One and her driver appear.
We watch with delight as he reverses into the bus.
She climbs on board to much laughter and cheer.
Write a report? But Ma'am, we're involved, can't be us!

The chastened female boss shrank away.
Back to the peace of deafening banter and fun.
Another few hours of earning, maximise our stay.
Finally, the Battersea serial dismissed with our copies of The Sun.

My first experience of aid on overtime was the print workers dispute at Wapping. I signed up to do a couple of shifts on my weekend off. We paraded at Battersea and after the head count made our way on to one of the angular green buses we used to use on aid.

The Wapping print dispute was an argument between the print unions and Rupert Murdoch about him relocating his newspaper production to a new more automated compound situated in the London Borough of Wapping. The dispute briefly became quite violent down at the new site and the police were called in to keep the Union picket line down to a manageable number and the rest of the mob of demonstrators and supporters were moved way back behind hastily constructed barriers at one end of The Highway.

There were a few nights of quite serious disorder, with lumps of concrete, paving slabs and bits of iron railings being launched at the police. But by the time Battersea officers started getting sent down there it was just a bit of shouting. Clearly there was potential for more trouble, so a budget was found from somewhere to send extra officers, like us, down to Wapping to keep order.

It just became a stand-off. There had been attempts to stop production and distribution of the newspapers from the new Wapping plant, but by that time, the police presence was overwhelming and the unions were restricted to their authorised six pickets outside the entrance and the rest had to make do with congregating somewhere on up on The Highway.

I did this duty on several occasions through the winter of 1986 until it all ended in early 1987. I remember it being cold, with a biting wind that whipped up and down the old narrow cobbled streets, where Jack the Ripper had once preyed on the vulnerable. These streets have now largely disappeared under the massive docklands redevelopment, which was just getting underway as we sat on our green coach, with the heater going full blast.

On one shift they actually told us to get out of our warm carriers and go on a foot patrol. Walk down The Highway, round into Cable Street, back up to The Highway, before back to our parked vehicles in Wapping Lane. Utterly pointless, but totally freezing. You didn't want to forget your gloves and scarf for that aid.

I was on a bus full of experienced officers. This was only a short time after the year long Miner's strike, so they were used to extended periods of time sat in a bus doing nothing, except earning. Someone always had a pack of cards to get a card school going. I don't know how, but I was always able to get some sleep on aid. Twenty to thirty minutes with my eyes closed, propped up against a stack of raincoats and boxes of snacks.

Talking of snacks. After about a week of aid being organised, the mobile canteen wagon (Teapot One) would turn up to feed us something hot. It's hard now to recollect anything other than this one memory of feeding down at Wapping. It was another bitterly cold night and we all waited our turn to queue up at the discreetly parked Teapot One. There was hot tea or coffee and what was billed as a Chilli Con Carne pie or pasty. As we waited in line I saw this mound of Chilli beef, beans and pastry on the floor just past the wagon. Before I had a chance to work it out, I was handed this scalding hot pie in a serviette. No cutlery or plate and just the one free hand as the other was clinging on to my coffee cup.

As I bit into the pie, the searing heat burnt my mouth, the pie came apart in my hand, scalding my fingers and I immediately dropped it, adding to the mound. Ah! Now I understood the dropped pies. Force feeding, always an experience.

I would have my eyes closed and be listening quite happily to the wonderful war stories my senior colleagues had from their weeks spent policing the Miners' strike. A year long strike. Wow! Wapping was a couple of months and I earned a few quid. It was easy to see how colleagues had bought houses, putting down a decent deposit to get a preferable mortgage rate. Their stories were both horrific and funny. The majority were seemingly about the jokes played on each other and more amusingly all the Constabularies encountered, while they were kept cooped up in buses and carriers, well away from the action because the County Senior Officers were too scared to use the Met.

Management could always be relied upon to both annoy and amuse. In the early hours of one shift, probably about 3am, an unmarked car drove down Wapping Lane towards our parked green bus. A few lads at the front recognised it as a senior officer's car and gave the rest of us the nod. Then, as the driver was trying to squeeze the car between two of the green buses, he reversed into ours with a dull thud. Well, we were all awake now!

There was a sort of extended pause before the door of our transport opened and a very young-looking female Superintendent climbed aboard. She was late twenties at most and certainly younger than the smiling group of 'old sweats' slouched in their seats smiling at her. She had a voice that could cut glass and should have been reading the news on the BBC at that time. Clearly the very minor damage only accident had flustered her a little and she seemed at a loss, at first, as to what to say.

"Right, well, I need one of you to report the minor accident my driver just had".

Nobody moved.

"Come on, you are all sitting here doing nothing, one of you needs to make a report"

After another extended silence, with her shifting from one foot to the other, hoping I imagine, that she wouldn't have to ask for a third time.

From the back of the bus came a low, deep but vaguely respectful voice. "Ma'am, with all due respect, we can't report your accident as we are all involved. I reckon we are 'persons concerned two to twelve' and as such no one on board can write it up".

"Well, that's just, well, you know, in these circumstances?", she was very flustered now.

"What, Ma'am? Is this a new sort of accident then?" The 'old sweats' were warming to the task now as another took her on.

"Oh, hang on Ma'am, I think I might have a bit of whiplash", they were off and running now, as the bus came alive with banter towards this young senior officer.

She realised she had lost all control as the cries went up throughout the bus and she quickly descended the steps and disappeared into the night. We never saw her again!

Ultimately this aid, like pretty much all aid, involved just sitting in a bus somewhere, trying to do anything to quell the boredom. Card schools, reading the newspaper or a book with a large amount of gossip and banter.

The aid to Wapping was a nice little earner, but it didn't last long. The bitterly cold weather did as much to keep order as anything our presence did. I think even the print worker unions could see that times were changing and there was a sad inevitability that their cause was lost.

The last few hours of the shift would really drag. Nothing was happening, most of the pickets and protesters had gone home to their warm beds. Our final task was to ensure that the early morning TNT distribution lorries were not hindered in getting out of the plant and speeding on their way with their cargo of daily newspapers. One of the wagons would dutifully stop and distribute copies of The Sun to us rank and file, and copies of The Times to the supervisors. It was then just the usual request to GT (The Scotland Yard radio channel for aid at Wapping) to let us be dismissed. Once clear to depart it was back to Battersea, booked off by the Sergeant and get home to enjoy what was left of my weekend.

A Heston Rave

A quiet night, a really slow and dull foot patrol.
In for refs. The usual kebab roll, hot sauce and a coffee.
A skipper rushes in. Ten level two trained is his goal.
We gather our kit and get on the bus. Better than walking in Battersea.

We blue light across the river in a carrier convoy
Destination Heston, a rave to address
At the Services car park we wait patiently to deploy
Let the party continue, far too many to process.

We watch a throng of humanity dance and sway.
Stay on the warm bus, as revellers stagger about.
Read the paper, crosswords and let the card school play.
Really shit music. Drugs are here, looking for the tout.

Boredom sets in as morning comes, we wait to be dismissed.
The clock clicks into overtime, as some party goers drift away.
Still the music thumps on, in the morning's light mist.
Cleared to depart. Let's see if someone wants to play?

A slow drive, we crawl through parked cars.
One brave soul kicks the carrier and screams abuse.
Side door open. In you come. Let's check his pars.
He was verbally warned and on Battersea Bridge, let loose!

Night Duty could sometimes be so deathly quiet and dull. We could have so many officers working that I would be on a foot patrol for the majority of the time. A driver would kindly pick you up to run you down to our preferred kebab shop at Clapham South, so you could get some refs but the night would drag and you were just hoping that something would happen.

On one quiet Night shift, something did. It relieved the boredom for a while and was such a strange and unique event that I remember it to this day.

The UK at the time of this story was in the grip of the rave culture. Large groups of people determined to have a good time. Dancing to heavily bass- influenced psychedelic type music, very much of their generation. I actually thought some of the music was alright, a bit repetitive and sampled for my taste, but some tunes had a bit of melody. The ravers wanted their parties to run all through the night and to find venues they would often just force their way into derelict or seemingly abandoned, buildings, warehouses, factories, storage facilities and barns. Organisers would fire up the sound systems and spread the word that an event was happening.

The police were slow to catch on to this new phenomenon as these events became quite frequent. The addition of a new drug of choice, ecstasy, made it clear that these 'raves' needed to be policed in some way. Several highly publicised deaths made it necessary for the police to step in to control and limit the spread of what was becoming a serious problem.

This brings me back to my quiet Night Duty shift at Battersea. I had got myself a kebab roll and was sitting chatting to colleagues in the canteen when our Duty Sergeant burst in with some news. The Yard wanted as many shield trained officers as possible to make their way down to Heston Services where it was believed an unlicensed rave was taking place in an abandoned warehouse behind the M4. The skipper had done some counting and there were ten of us who were Level Two shield trained. We also, by complete coincidence, had a carrier parked in the yard, fully kitted with shields and all the rest of the paraphernalia you would expect, which was required for some aid the following day.

To be Level Two shield trained meant that you had been to the shield training school in Hounslow every four months or so, to have petrol bombs thrown at you and deal with a violent man wearing a wolf's head mask in an enclosed space. The final element of the training was a 500-metre shield run in full kit in under two minutes and forty-five seconds. During the time there, they used wooden blocks to throw at us and tennis balls if there were horses deployed. You were more likely to be trampled by a horse than injured by anything else, but it was a fun two days in this false town urban environment that had been created. Hounslow riot village was built on some land away from other buildings and people's dwellings. Then they built a new housing estate close by and we had to stop throwing petrol bombs and shouting at each other by early evening. I suspect it got progressively more difficult to run the Hounslow site, so now everything that used to happen there, happens at Gravesend in Kent.

Before we could grab our kit and get in the carrier, we needed the permission of the Duty Officer. He was concerned that he was losing a Sergeant and ten Constables from his Night Duty roster of troops. He still had the Area Car, a van and two other patrol vehicles and he could always wake up the Night Duty CID. This was our 'Sit Rep' Governor, and I think he was always thinking we were trying to pull a stroke or have him over in some way.

The Sergeant showed the boss the message from Information room at the Yard and finally he gave his permission for us to get assigned. The Yard set up a separate channel and assigned us to attend, call sign Whisky Alpha Three Zero. They advised that Wandsworth and Tooting were both sending carriers and that they would come to our station. Once gathered, we should deploy to Heston Services in convoy.

My colleague with the unnerving laugh was driving and we disappeared down to the locker room to get our black holdalls full of our Level Two kit. A flame-retardant one-piece boiler suit, that you wore over your normal uniform. Some knee and shin guards that attached with Velcro, elbow pads, a pair of steel toe capped boots and a NATO issue crash helmet with a visor. Most officers supplemented this issued kit with additional trousers, tops and other flexible shin guards. All zipped up in a big black holdall, stored above your locker.

Back in the yard we loaded up. Our driver kicked the tyres and we waited for our colleagues from Wandsworth and Tooting to arrive. A short while later our three carriers set off in convoy, blue lights on as we sped over Battersea Bridge and headed west towards the M4. It was genuinely exciting! We didn't really know what we were going to be faced with, but that was pretty much the norm on a day-to-day basis anyway. A Chief Inspector from the local ground had been turfed out of bed and on his instruction, we were to park up at the services.

When we arrived, it was chaos. As we pulled off the motorway we could see cars had been parked on the hard shoulder of the M4. The services were just as bad, littered with poorly parked cars. Bronze (the local Chief Inspector) had quickly got some traffic officers out of their lair and they were busy ticketing and removing all the vehicles from the M4 to a car pound in Charlton, south-east London. This was better than sex to a black rat! (Traffic Officer).

Our three carriers parked up line astern, behind another eight to ten from all over London. It was a quiet night everywhere then; well except Heston! We began changing into our riot gear, only for Bronze to decide on an alternative strategy. He told us to wait in our vehicles and let the rave subside of its own accord. Avoid confrontation and no stop and searches. I think all the officers were just too tired on our respective Night Duties to be that bothered. Chances are we were going to be earning out of it and from my own perspective being sat in a warm carrier talking bollocks was preferable to patrolling the dead streets of Battersea in the cold.

The Sergeant allowed someone to go and get a coffee from the service area. He came back beaming from ear to ear. The services at Heston were so glad of our presence that teas, coffees and snacks were complimentary. Really? There followed a steady stream of officers into the service shop to pretty much empty it of stock during the next few hours. Someone on board had a transistor radio that tried to compete with the cacophony of sound coming from the building hosting this impromptu rave. You could close your eyes and try and get some sleep, but the heavy bass of the music shook you awake.

We just sat there as the night wore on and the first glimpses of the Sunday morning's dawn were witnessed. The occasional person or group from the rave staggered past, vaguely aware that there were about 100 police officers watching and waiting. A brave soul came up to our driver and beckoned for him to lower his window. *"This will be good"*, I thought.

"Excuse me officer I don't seem to be able to find my car".

"Where did you park it, sir?", always polite.

"On the hard shoulder of the motorway, there wasn't any room in the services car park".

"That would have been removed by one of our traffic officers, as it's illegal to park on the hard shoulder of a motorway", still polite.

"Oh! but there were loads of cars parked there, we thought it would be alright, it being a Saturday night".

"No sir, always illegal".

"Where would it have been taken then?"

Knowing exactly where all the vehicles had been taken, our driver took a slow long sharp intake of breath, then he spoke.

"They will all have gone to the vehicle pound at Charlton. You will have to attend in person with identification, proof of ownership and the fee for its recovery. Don't leave it too long, they charge by the day for storage", polite, informative and truthful.

"But, Charlton, that's miles away, how do we get there? We came down here from Swindon!"

That was it. My driver couldn't hold it any longer and gave one of the most perfect of his deep maniacal laughs on hearing this party goer's predicament.

Our Sergeant stepped out of the carrier and took over from our driver. He provided an address, phone number and opening hours of the pound at Charlton and the bemused 'raver' drifted away.

Having eaten everything available from the services and being officially on overtime we were all a bit bored now and we persuaded the Sergeant to ask if we could be dismissed. The Chief Inspector was getting similar requests from all the other carriers, who just like us were bored, tired and wanted to go home. Almost simultaneously the music suddenly stopped and with it the awful incessant bass boom.

This was the cue for the weary Chief Inspector to give the order for us to be dismissed. Our driver found a gap at the back of the services that he could squeeze the carrier through and off we went. Very quickly we discovered the other area where all those attending the spontaneous party had parked their vehicles. It was heaving with cars abandoned on pavements and verges and we had to crawl through at walking pace.

The streets were now filled with all the people returning to their cars and we had to move even slower to get through. Just as we were at the last few vehicles before the roads opened up, I heard a dull thud to the side of our vehicle. Our driver stopped immediately, as a colleague in the 'jump' seat prepared to open the side door.

"That bloke in the waistcoat kicked the van as we passed", our driver smiled.

He reversed until we were alongside the frozen waistcoat. The side door was slid open.

Two pairs of hands reached out grabbed him and lifted him into the van. The door slid closed and we were off.

Our morning guest was sat on the floor in the rear of the bus, with us all staring down at him.

The Sergeant turned around from his front passenger seat and asked for the guest's details.

As these were given and checks were performed I noticed that all he had on was this dark coloured waistcoat over his bare upper torso. It had little stars and representations of the planets on it. Far out!

It was made clear that he was now under arrest for criminal damage to our police vehicle, which I presume ruined his evening.

As we got back on to the Bath Road and then A4 towards Hammersmith and Chelsea, a decision was made between our skipper and driver. As much as overtime was actively sought, they were both tired after a week of Nights and neither fancied the lengthy processing that a charge of criminal damage would necessitate. Plus, how would anyone know what damage had been caused when comparing it to all the other dents and scrapes already present.

As the carrier turned from the embankment on to Battersea Bridge the skipper turned to the weary passenger.

"Right mate. Never a good idea to kick a carrier full of police officers. But in the interests of your future, we won't be prosecuting you. We have decided to use our discretion in this matter and deal with it by way of a verbal warning. You are therefore de-arrested. Don't do it again. Do you understand?"

"Err! Yes, thank you officer".

The driver stopped the van at the apex of Battersea Bridge, the side door was slid open, out he got, door slid shut and we just left him there on that cold crisp Sunday morning, at the top of Battersea Bridge in little more than his hippy waistcoat.

Back at the Nick, some notes were made to cover the redistribution of the reveller and we were booked off with four hours in black (time and a third overtime) and headed off home for some sleep.

Whisky One

The flagship vehicle of our response.
License to roam and cherry pick calls.
A posting on the car, please, just once?
After a month of this, all other work palls.

Mains set radio and the Met sound wail.
A bigger, faster car to operate.
Major calls, its who the controllers hail.
Whisky One on scene, now giving an update.

Six weeks of residential Hendon training.
Constant theory and practical tests.
Get through phase one, but keep on learning.
Pass or fail? On your final drive it rests.

Cracked the emergency call, now the pursuit.
After forty-five minutes the time has gone.
Back to Hendon please. You know the route.
A high scoring pass, a job well done.

Return to Borough with a spring in my stride.
The Duties Sergeant awards me a month on Whisky One.
Pushing the limit, all my training applied.
Are you an Advanced Driver? No mate, a Class One!

There was a well-established pecking order on the Relief for courses. One of the most keenly contested of these was the Standard Driving Course. It all came down to seniority of service, matched by a determination to stay on the Relief. There were a few candidates ahead of me in the queue, but this got smaller when people moved on and suddenly I was near to the top.

I had only passed my driving test in the August of 1987, so I knew that I could do with a little bit of driving experience. When I finally got given a course in the spring of 1989, this was not seen by my instructor as a limitation, but rather a bonus. In his words.

"Not too many bad habits then!"

The Standard Driving Course I undertook was a three-week, instructed, continual assessment. You were split into a syndicate of three people. In my team was an officer from Wimbledon and one from Sutton. After the initial Hendon start, the subsequent days we met at Mitcham Police Station. At that time, I was living in Mitcham. This arrangement suited all of us and our instructor, a retired police officer, back as a civilian driving instructor lived in Worcester Park, so he was happy too.

There followed three weeks of learning to drive to 'The System'. It's now embedded in my brain.

"The System of car control is a system or drill, each feature of which, is considered, in sequence, by the driver at the approach to any hazard".

Following the Roadcraft Driving Manual you employ a strategy to drive in a manner that is safe, systematic and smooth, but you still need to make good progress.

All three of us passed the course and were returned to our respective Boroughs as Standard Drivers. Suddenly my days of walking the beat would become a rarity and I would be able to drive the smaller powered police vehicles. The Duties Sergeant gave me a month of driving one of the patrol vehicles, as a reward for passing my course.

As with everything, there is the desire for progression and for me, I had decided uniform Relief work was what I enjoyed. Not for me the crime squad, leading to being a fully-fledged Detective in the CID. Neither specialism in Traffic nor the recently formed TSG, who were to be a permanent replacement to the District sourced DSU. I was committed to staying on the Relief and as a consequence I was soon in line for my next course.

The van! You had to go to Hendon to complete the van driving course. The police van at that time was the Leyland Sherpa, rear wheel drive, so when you gave it the beans, you could drift it round corners in the wet. Years later I learned that you could drift a carrier too, but on that day, drifting a carrier full of officers sideways in Battersea Church Road was not by design, just my heavy right foot!

The main criterion for passing the van course was being able to reverse it into a succession of tight parking spaces, with as few shunts as possible to leave it parallel parked without needing a taxi to get you to the curb. I always loved driving the van. It was fitted with a single rotating blue light on the roof, but without the familiar two-tone siren you got in the Area Car. I was authorised to answer emergency calls, treat red lights as give ways and could put on the blue light. The only noise to announce your presence to other motorists was the horn of the vehicle and additionally the operator could hold down a switch which activated a bell that went 'dring dring' as you sped along. Professional stuff!

I had my first 'POLACC' (police vehicle involved in an accident) driving the van. In my service I had more than several 'POLACC'S' but this was my first and I shall explain the circumstances.

I had an operator and it was at the start of a Night Duty shift. We were travelling west along Battersea Park Road, just by The Clockhouse pub. A call came over the radio of a colleague needing urgent assistance in Battersea Rise at the junction with St. John's Road.

I gunned the engine, put the light on and my operator did his thing with the 'dring dring'.

I knew from experience that as you approach the junction with Battersea Bridge Road and Latchmere Road there is zero vision into Battersea Bridge Road on your right. I slowed the van almost to a stop as the lights for us to proceed were red. As we got within about ten yards of the stop line the lights changed from red to green in our favour. I knocked the engine down a cog and accelerated. At that moment a Citroen 2CV entered the junction from Battersea Bridge Road, heading South into Latchmere Road. I had no time to react and we broadsided the Citroen.

The little French car came apart like one of those 'clown' cars you used to see at the circus. All the doors, panels and wheels came off and the driver was left effectively sitting in the road in his seat holding a steering wheel. There was debris everywhere. The van had a minor paint scrape to the front grill. Fortunately, no one was hurt and sufficient units had got to my colleague in Battersea Rise to assist him.

The driver of the Citroen was taken to hospital as a precaution and a Traffic Sergeant attended and took statements from myself, my operator colleague and then a statement from the other driver at hospital. As far as I was concerned I had waited until the lights changed to green in my favour and accelerated through the stop line legally. The Citroen had gone through on red, hence the accident was his fault, end of.

Not according to the other driver, who was clear in his recollection that it had been the police van driven by me that had gone through the lights on red and the collision was therefore my fault. All information was collated and sent to the process section and CPS to decide. I, in the meantime, was suspended from driving, pending the outcome.

I spent a wonderful month operating the Area Car with my good friend who had thrown the hand grenade at our Duty Officer.

These things take time to be processed and I don't remember exactly how long it took for a decision to be arrived at, so all I could do was to carry on working and wait. I got a note from the Duty Officer one morning in my pigeonhole to come and see him. I presumed he had a 'Situation Report' for me!

Indeed, he did. The CPS had decided to prosecute me for Dangerous Driving and as such he needed to serve me with a Regulation Seven notice, (Form 163) to that effect. Blimey! That focuses the mind. On the Relief I was quite blasé and untouched by this, but inside I was really worried. I didn't believe I had done anything wrong. The official paperwork arrived the following week, with a summons for me to attend Wells Street Magistrates Court in a couple of month's time. Wells Street Magistrates Court was just off Oxford Street in Central London and I used to give evidence there on a regular basis. There was one particular Stipendiary Magistrate who used to rip you apart if you made any sort of mistake and that was as a prosecuting witness.

"As long as I don't get him", I thought.

Let me just pause this story to talk about attending Court for a moment. As an officer you get to attend Court quite often in your service to give evidence. I was always nervous going to Court. It's like a theatre, it's serious and the stakes are high. You are there to give your evidence and invariably up against a selection of people and characters who know far more about the law than you do.

At Hendon during our training there was a mock Court set up. This was where you learned about some of the traditions and protocol of your role at Court. The expectations of you as a police officer as you present yourself and give your evidence. The faux Court allowed you to get the feel for how it was going to be in a real Court. To stand in the witness box, swear your oath, before announcing and introducing yourself to the judge. Understanding what to call the judges was imparted too, as you deliver your evidence in a clear and loud voice, remembering to call them Your Worship (Magistrates), Your Honour (Crown Court) or My Lord (High Court).

One seasoned 'Old Sweat' on the Relief made it perfectly clear that giving evidence was simple and that to prevent coming unstuck by a clever defence question you stick to a very straight forward rule. Once you have introduced yourself, which consisted of your rank, name and the station to which you were attached there was only ever the need to say three things in answer to the questions posed. "Yes", "No" or 'I don't know". Nothing more. Never try and engage with them or give anything else. Stick to that principle and you will be ok was his philosophy.

As I said, Court is a theatre, where great orators thrive and those without confidence and who are full of nerves can struggle. There were always one or two officers I worked with and watched give evidence, who had the natural ability to perform. To be able to provide their evidence in a calm almost nonchalantly professional way. They were also seldom rattled under cross examination by the defence councils and clearly hadn't heeded the yes, no, or I don't know rule. They had the natural charisma and confidence to take on the wigged specialists. One example I remember…..

Defence: "I put it to you Officer, that you could not possibly have seen that the suspect was my client from your concealed position so far away.

Officer: Nothing from him, apart from a glance at the judge with a face that said, "*I'll hold my council until he actually asks me a question*".

Defence: "Perhaps you can tell us here today at what distance you would estimate you were from the scene of this crime?"

Officer: Just the perfect length of a pause before he lifts his head and looks up at the judge. "I was between 100 and 120 yards from where the incident took place, Your Worship." (Magistrates Court).

Defence: "You state in your evidence that you clearly saw my client from that distance, bearing in mind that it was at night and the street lighting at that location was poor?"

Officer: (In no way troubled). Yes, Your Worship.

Defence: "Oh! Really Officer. Well, you must have particularly good eyesight?"

Officer: (Still very relaxed and calm). Yes, Your Worship.

Defence: "Do you wear any form of corrective lenses or spectacles or is your eyesight in any way impaired?"

Officer: No, Your Worship.

Defence: Well if that also means you haven't had any sort of eyesight test or check-up recently; how do you know how good your eyesight is? I mean, how far do you think you can see at night?

Officer: A slightly longer pause, as if he was thinking how to answer this question, but he knew straight away what he was going to say. He was just toying with the defence.

"Well now, (a brilliantly timed pause), on a clear night, like the evening of this incident, I can see the moon! Your Worship!"

Then he did what so many others would have failed to do. He kept his features totally deadpan, as he looked at the judge.

Defence: "Yes thank you Officer, nothing further", and the defence sat down, just a little bit ruffled.

The officer kept his composure as he walked smartly from the witness box and out of the Court. I suspect he was very probably, in the eyes of the judge, right on the brink of flippancy or possible contempt or both. But it was his very real charm and flamboyance in the box that saw him walk quickly and safely from the crucible of the Court.

Anyway, back to my traffic matter and being on the other side of the fence in Court.

By the time the court case came around I had a Federation Representative to assist me and legal counsel arranged through him. On the morning of the case a good half dozen members of the Relief attended as well. Oh, and two goons from complaints were at the back of the Court, circling like hungry sharks.

There is nothing that can prepare you for 'gripping the rail' at Court. Even though it was only a traffic matter, I was bricking it. I had been on duty, doing my job, going to assist a colleague and as far as I was concerned the other driver had jumped a red light. But that's not how the prosecution saw things.

I stood as the Magistrate came into the Court. "*Oh! Bollocks!*", it was the one that usually tore us a new one. I remained standing while the rest of the Court settled. I gave my name and then sat while the CPS prosecutor stood to give brief facts of the case.

As he announced that I was an on-duty police officer at the time of the alleged offence, the Magistrate interrupted him.

"Let me just stop you there. This is a serving police officer, on duty at the time?"

"Yes sir".

"I am not having serving police officers in the dock of my Court", then beckoning to me,

"Officer, please come and take a seat next to your defence council".

As I walked from the dock down to the chair next to my barrister I was stunned by this development.

"Continue!"

The CPS chap then described the circumstances of the collision. He may have neglected to mention that I was at the time driving a marked police van and had just answered an emergency call from a colleague seeking urgent assistance.

An independent witness had been discovered by the Traffic Sergeant on the night of the incident. He had been coming out of The Latchmere Public House and claimed to have seen the entire thing. However, in his evidence he stated, "I turned to see the accident". Not exactly what was in his statement, where he claimed to have witnessed the whole thing. What? So, having told the Sergeant in his statement he saw the lights change and the police van career through them on a red light, he then made the mistake of saying in the witness box that he had to turn to see the coming together of the two vehicles. Oops!

My defence man rose to his feet and annihilated the witness. By the time he was finished, the witness didn't know which way was up!

My turn. I nervously stood in the witness box and gave the oath. I took the court through my version of events. I described my location and then what caused me to put on the blue light and answer the assistance call. That's when the Magistrate stopped me. As I looked up at him, my fear rose. I could see he had availed himself of a 'Geographia' map book of London, similar to the ones we carried in our vehicles and was studying the roads described in the case.

"If I might interrupt, Officer. You were on duty, driving a marked police vehicle"?

"Yes, Your Worship".

"You took an urgent call to aid a colleague in some sort of trouble?'

"Yes, Your Worship".

'What was your intended route to this, Officer?" I could see the

Magistrate was marking the map book with his finger.

"Sir, I was going to continue west along Battersea Park Road, then turn left into Falcon Road all the way down to the junction with Lavender Hill and St. John's Hill. Straight across this junction into St. John's Road and at the end is Battersea Rise, where my colleague was needing assistance, Your Worship".

I thanked my stars that I had a good working knowledge of all the streets of Battersea Division.

"Thank you, Officer, that's excellent. I don't need to hear any more. Please re-join your council." He waited for me to return to my seat before addressing the CPS chap.

"I'm not having this. You bring before me a serving police officer, on duty, performing his duties. Your independent witness is discredited and clearly did not witness the actual accident. I do not expect to see hard working and diligent officers being prosecuted when they clearly have no case to answer. Case dismissed; costs awarded to the defence". With that he stood and was gone before we had all risen to our feet.

"*Blimey that was a turn up!*" I stood in stunned silence while the CPS clerk noisily gathered his papers together. My defence man shook my hand as I thanked him. I turned around to my muckers at the back of the Court who were on their feet smiling and giving me the thumbs up. The two complaints boys slithered away without a word.

One of the Relief skippers was there and he immediately informed me that I was reinstated to driving duties and also that I was one 'Lucky Fucker'.

As I said, I had many 'POLACC'S' in the police and a lot of them were down to me. But this one in the van wasn't.

Before I finish talking about Wells Street Magistrates Court, there was another memorable occasion there. I was one of four officers called to give evidence about an affray at some location. Three constables and one of our skippers. We'd all been on scene and involved in the three suspects being arrested and made copious notes of the incident and our arrests.

When you get to Court, usually about 9.30am, there is a Police Room, where officers called to Court can sit and relax, have a hot drink and make use of a phone to urgently call the station to bring anything to Court that might have been overlooked and is needed NOW!

The CPS prosecutor is usually there to check that all the police and other witnesses have turned up and to discuss anything that they are unsure of.

Before the case gets underway there is loads of legal stuff that has to be sorted. Inevitably you end up waiting a long time at Court, while nothing seemingly happens. This was just such a day and we sat and had a brew, read the papers and waited. The Courts usually start at about 10 – 10.30 am and run until lunch at 12.30 – 1pm. As the clock ticked closer to lunch our CPS lady returned to the

Police Room with news.

"I am pretty sure they are going to change their plea to guilty", she looked around at us.

A change of plea was a common thing at this late stage of proceedings, so we always half expected it.

"Can we go then?" our skipper asked, just checking that we were now dismissed from Court.

"Well, we haven't had a chance for them to officially enter a change of plea, so it's a formality, but if you can just hang around until after lunch. Once we have the change of plea in front of the Magistrate, we can let you all go. If you can be back here for 2pm please", and with that she was gone.

I never really worked out whose fault it was. The prosecutor for pretty much telling us we were dismissed. My colleague, suggesting a beer in the pub over the road or the rest of us for going along with it and agreeing to have a pint.

The pub was a beautiful old Victorian place called The Champion, at that time run by the Samuel Smiths brewery from Tadcaster, Yorkshire. It had an ornate wooden interior with wonderful stained-glass windows.

Four pints of Sam Smith's best bitter arrived at our table, courtesy of our skipper and we settled into the comfortable environment to enjoy our ale. Four identically clad police officers, sat in a pub opposite Wells Street Magistrates Court in half blues. (half blues was what you wore on public transport on your way to wherever. It was uniform trousers, white shirt, sometimes a tie, all concealed by a civilian jacket).

We were an incredibly polite and fastidious group and each of us quite rightly bought a round, as we sampled some pub sandwiches to go with our beer. At about 1.50pm we had got through our four pints each and swayed back to the Court to be officially dismissed.

"Where have you been?" the CPS lady exclaimed as we crashed through the door into the Police Room.

"Lunch", we all replied in unison. I think one of us belched too.

"Well get some coffee on and eat some mints, because they have decided to go Not Guilty and you are going to have to give evidence. It smells like a brewery in here".

"Fuck".

"Yes, exactly." She pointed to one of my bemused colleagues. "You'll be first. The court starts in five minutes", she then disappeared.

The mists of time have made that afternoon a bit of a blur. That, and the four pints of Sam Smiths. I do know we all gave evidence. I do know the whole Court must have been aware we were pissed. It was the same Stipendiary Magistrate who had dismissed my driving matter. He was such a fearsome character; I can't believe we got away with it. There are passing moments when I recall crunching down a packet of Trebor Extra Strong mints in the waiting area outside the Court, immediately prior to being called to give evidence. Being asked a direct question by the defence and him having to repeat it because I simply didn't understand what he was saying. None of us stayed in the court room after having given our evidence because of the aroma of beer around us.

We returned to the Police Room, drinking strong coffee waiting for the result. The CPS lady finally arrived.

"I don't quite know how we did that. I was convinced the case would be dismissed when you tripped up the steps into the witness box and crashed into the bible and oath cards", pointing at a colleague.

The laughter was deafening. Part of me wished I'd stayed in the court after giving my evidence, to see that. But then the laughter I was exhibiting now would have been in the court room, so probably best I wasn't.

"Somehow the defence dropped the ball and didn't realise the state you were all in and the Magistrate, who I am convinced did know, found them guilty, then winked at me as he left the court. Good afternoon gentlemen!" and with that she was gone.

Court. Always a fun time!

Not long after I had passed my van course I was tasked with one of the more bizarre occasions when I have attended Court. It wasn't my case; I was simply the person driving the van (Whisky Alpha Two) that particular Early Turn.

"Whisky Alpha Two, can you return to Whisky Alpha so we can have a chat? Over".

"Received, over".

Back at the station the controller smiled as he gave me my task. I actually thought it was a wind up at first. Freshly qualified to drive the van and they hand me this job. Got to be a wind up! But no, it wasn't.

I was to find a physically strong operator from the canteen. Go to the bulky property store at Charlton and pick up a large wardrobe. Take this wardrobe to Number One Court at The Old Bailey, where the judge would like it visible in the court for tomorrow please. The large item of furniture had been moved to the transit area of the property store and they were expecting me. You can see why I thought that it was obviously a wind up! But let me give some background.

There was a well known couple who lived on our patch. They both liked a drink and most weekends the husband liked to give his wife a good pasting when he got back from the pub. We were constantly there to arrest him for another assault on his wife. She gave as good as she got and would often throw knives, saucepans, plates of food, or anything not nailed down at him, when she herself was in a drunken fury. Most officers were familiar with them and it was almost a 'right of passage' to arrest one or other, whilst a probationary officer.

One day another Relief on duty were called to their address. The officers were confronted by the steaming drunk female, who was completely incoherent. A swift search of the premises revealed the apparently lifeless body of her husband on their bed, face down, with a large, incredibly heavy, oak and walnut, free-standing wardrobe on top of him.

I don't know much of the circumstances, as I said, it wasn't my case but this was what was believed to have happened. As the assaults on the female increased in regularity and ferocity she decided, finally, that she'd had enough. It was supposed, that she had loaded the wardrobe with more and more clothing and blankets. Depositing large boxes on the top of it and hanging clothes off the doors. It must have taken her a while and was completely premeditated. After one particularly vicious assault her husband had fallen asleep on the bed. It was claimed that she had shifted enough weight on to the wardrobe as to change its centre of gravity. The faintest of pulls from her with both doors open, was sufficient to send the great wooden piece of furniture crashing down on top of her sleeping husband. It both crushed and asphyxiated him and afterwards she got royally drunk, then called the police to say her husband was dead.

One of the young officers on scene that morning decided in his wisdom to arrest her for murder, just on the off chance. The CID attended and as they too sniffed something suspicious about the circumstances they were furious to discover a uniform had already nicked her. As the investigation commenced the exhibits officer tagged the wardrobe and all its contents as evidence and after SOCO had finished with it, off it went to the bulky property store at Charlton. And that's where I came in.

I'd never been to the store at Charlton before but my enormous colleague, perched on the seat next to me had, so we found it fairly easily. There was indeed a welcoming committee to greet us on arrival and with one of their storemen, the three of us manhandled the wardrobe into the rear of the van. We then loaded four large property bags full of clothing and blankets and two large cardboard boxes of old magazines that had been both in and on the wardrobe at the time of the alleged offence.

Off we went to the Old Bailey. The Central Criminal Court, commonly called The Old Bailey because of the street it's in, is situated in the City of London, just behind St. Paul's Cathedral. We drove through the Blackwall tunnel to get North of the river and then headed West towards the City.

There are large gates at the old frontage of the court and we were buzzed in when we explained who we were. Somehow, with additional help from one of the gaolers at the court we got the wardrobe out of the van and up the steps to the foyer and cells area.

I didn't know it, but fortunately there is a lift to get from the cells up to the Courts. After some heaving and shoving with accompanying swearing we got the thing in the lift and up to the corridor outside of Court Number One. The court wasn't sitting, so we opened the doors to see where we could put the bloody wardrobe (and all the clothes and blankets).

Court Number One at The Old Bailey is very grand. Wooden panels around the walls and there are intricate carvings on the panels in front of the viewing gallery. The wooden benches are inlaid with green leather padding with gold embossed crests on them. Above the panels, the upper portions of the walls and ceiling are pure white plaster domes and arches, with decorative plasterwork. It is an impressive room, within an equally impressive and famous building.

At the back of the court, behind and to the left of the defendant's dock there was a wooden panelled pillar. I judged the distance between this pillar and the far wall to be about the same width as the wardrobe. Back out in the corridor we again sought the help of a couple of other officers and between all of us, we manoeuvred the bulky wooden armoire into the court room and wedged it between the pillar and the wall. I walked around to the front and had a look. Then I walked down towards the front of the court and looked at it from where the Judge would see it. By pure fluke, the thing matched the panelled walls. It looked like it belonged there, perhaps not as highly polished, but the same warm nutty brown, aged colour.

I thanked the assisting officers. My 'oppo' and I put the boxes on the top and the bags of clothing inside the wardrobe, closed the door and returned to the cellblock area.

We made slow progress back to Battersea, still slightly bemused as to what we had just done. It was the last I saw of that wardrobe. Like I said, it wasn't my case and I was simply delivering some bulky evidential property. I was never asked to collect it and I don't recall anyone ever talking to me about collecting it. I gave evidence several times at The Old Bailey, but never in Number One court. I always forgot to pop in to check. I do wonder if it's still there?

So that's the van driving all sorted then.

These things were like stepping stones. You needed to be a Standard Driver, then a Van Driver before being selected for the one everyone wanted, Advanced Driver! Like my previous courses there were people on the Relief who were ahead of me in the queue for an Advanced Driving Course. But you bide your time, keep working hard to at least be in consideration for when a course comes along. Management has to make hard decisions. One of the considerations when determining an Advanced Course was to ensure that the freshly qualified driver gave at least two years of service to the Relief after returning successfully from Hendon. That seemed a reasonable return to me and I wanted to stay on the Relief anyway.

Sometimes, when courses were few and far between there would be a check test drive off between the best three candidates. A qualified Advanced Driver on Borough would conduct the driving test and make his decision. I saw that happen to the allocation of the course before mine.

When the next course came around I was in consideration for it. It appeared at short notice as a cancellation from another Borough. As a consequence, I was the only person that was available with no annual leave, complaints or Court commitments for the next six weeks, which was very rare for me. Bloody hell that's a stroke of luck, the course was mine.

Six weeks of Advanced Driver training at The Metropolitan Police Driving School, Hendon. At that time the course offered accommodation in the recruit blocks, which was fortunate, because I lived at the southern end of the Northern Line. It was a uniformed course and each morning there was a parade with inspection. Dress of the day was posted on the wall at the entrance to the driving school and everyone was to comply.

Not having to travel up to Hendon on a daily basis was the key. After a full day driving I would not have relished a two-hour journey home on the tube. The course was hard, as it should be. You are going to be driving on occasion, well above the speed limit and treating things like traffic signals as give-ways. You will also be trained to pursue suspects who fail to stop or try to evade police.

Similar to the standard course you were split into syndicates of three, with an instructor. Initially you were working towards getting through the phase one test at the end of week two. This test was conducted by one of the examiners and it was a hurdle that not everyone managed. I made it.

Phase two of the course was when it got really hard. A bigger car with the introduction of full commentary. Giving the instructor as much information about your drive as you flew around the roads of North London and the Home Counties in an unmarked three litre Vauxhall Senator. Commentary when you are driving takes time to learn, but eventually it becomes second nature to literally say what you see. You also get to do the first part of 'bandit training'. Following and trying not to lose an instructor who is driving an identical car to the one you are in.

Bandit training is all about your driving plan. Trying to second guess what the bandit is going to do. Don't get too close, because you won't be able to react to him. But if he gets too far, you'll lose him. Each day got tougher as you honed your skills in fast driving to be able to get to emergencies and your pursuit training, to bring cars failing to comply to a safe stop. In amongst all of this was a collection of available, miscellaneous vehicles you would be check tested on. I got most of them; the JCB wasn't working and James Bond had nicked the Aston, again! (git). But I went through Carriers, Landrovers, 52-seater Coach and reversing an articulated lorry.

Weeks five and six were really long days. Each of the three of us in the car would be doing a full forty-five-minute drive in the morning, with full discussions after each one. Then another similar long drive in the afternoon. We did a night run up to Grafham Water in Cambridgeshire, to see how we coped without street lighting. It was all building to the last day of the course. The final drive.

You have been constantly assessed on the course and they have an idea of what mark you are going to get. It's up to you on the final drive to, hopefully, exceed their expectations. My emergency call was a blur and I felt I had done myself justice as we parked up and met with the other vehicle, which would be my 'bandit' car. Off we went, another forty-five minutes that went by in the blink of an eye. Notable in my memory for one particularly good, high-speed exit from a motorway and onto the slip road. The bandit must have thought he had me! Eventually my examiner told me the assessment was at an end. He asked me to take him back to Bushy Police Sports Ground, where we would have a full debrief of my drives.

You needed to get above 75% throughout the course to pass and be a qualified Advanced Driver. Candidates exceeding 85% would be given Class One status. I was so nervous as we sat down with a coffee looking out over the sports pitches at Bushy from the lounge bar. My instructor was sat next to me as the examiner went through his notes. He was quite matter of fact and went through our route for the emergency call and highlighted areas that impressed him, while giving little pointers as to what he may have done differently.

So far so good. Then on to the 'bandit' part. Again, he was listing things that he liked. He made mention of the high-speed exit from the motorway that I had thought was good. And he did too! We got to the end of his summary and I really didn't know.

"I think you acquitted yourself well and you gave me two good drives. I have given you 89%".

He may have carried on talking but I wasn't listening. *"89%, have it! Class One!"* was all I could think.

In the grand scheme of things, it was just a driving course. But in April 1991 I became a Class One Hendon Trained Advanced Police Driver. I was immediately given a month's posting, driving Whisky One back at Battersea and I loved every second of it. One operator I had during that first posting commented that it was like being in a life sized Scalextric as we hurtled around the streets of Battersea and beyond.

As the years went by I had my fair share of POLACC's driving Whisky One, culminating in one that gained me fame and notoriety on Trinity Road in Wandsworth. But more of that story later.

When someone who I had not seen for a while asked me in the canteen if I was now an Advanced Driver, I had my answer ready.

"Nah! Mate, I'm a Class One!

Railway!

Kids on the station platform at Battersea Park Road.
Whisky One, we'll take it. Any more information?
Juveniles train surfing. It makes the blood run cold.
Give it some 'Bugle' to get to the station.

Up the stairs, people milling about, the guard is crouched down.
Train at the station. The driver looks dazed.
A ten-year-old lad has gone under the train.
Restore order, power off. Try to remain unfazed.

Train moved back. Await power off confirmation.
I can see bits of him, some clothes, a single trainer.
On the platform another lad, a shivering wreck, gives us information.
Power is off. We close the whole station to be safer.

The Duty Officer wants a situation report.
Colleagues are sent to the parents.
There were bits of this lad everywhere, too much to sort.
Took the other boy home to his mum, wearing the jacket I'd lent.

The victim's mum is at his mate's address as we attend.
There is anger, blame and recrimination towards the other.
This poor little child is broken, difficult to mend.
Afterwards we sit in silence. Numb! But not like a mother.

Battersea's ground was bisected by numerous railway lines all merging together at Clapham Junction. As I have already mentioned, we were constantly involved with jobs both on or near the railway. In addition to the main Clapham Junction Station, we had the smaller stations in Queenstown Road and Battersea Park Road, both at the Eastern edge of our ground.

The overriding rule from everyone I worked with is you NEVER go on the railway line until you have it confirmed that the power is off. If a suspect you are chasing wants to run across the twelve or so parallel sets of tracks to evade capture, then let him go. Getting the power turned off wasn't easy and could take a while. You just had to wait, then double check before you ventured on to the lines.

Trains today are different to how they were when this horrible tragedy occurred. Back then it was the so called 'slam door' style carriages. The ones where people would still be trying to open the doors and clamber aboard, ignoring the shrill blasts of the whistle from the station guards, as the train was picking up speed leaving the station. There were some pretty awful accidents.

Another feature of this style of train, was a narrow wooden running board or ledge that ran under each of the doors, designed to ease exit and entry; but when the train was stationary. For a brief period, we had a spate of young children getting on to the platforms of the stations on our Borough and jumping on to these running boards, as the train was pulling in. This incredibly dangerous bit of fun came to be known as 'Train Surfing' and it was a craze that was always going to lead to an horrific accident.

Nothing prepares you for some of the awful things you see as a police officer. The daily horrors of what officers have to deal with on a tour of duty. Those horrific events that only increase in number with experience. They have certainly never left me. There are simply too many things that you cannot unsee. It affects you, and those around you. But, at the time, the training you have been given kicks in and you do whatever you can, to deal with the situation.

We took the call to the report of kids on the line. We received this information while in the canteen at the station. We screamed out of the yard, down Battersea Bridge Road and hammered along Prince of Wales Drive to Queen's Circus with all the lights and noise going. Third exit off the roundabout, then left at the lights and stop outside Battersea Park Station entrance. It's an elevated section of line at this point, so you get into the ticket office then climb the stairs to the platforms. We ran up the stairs to be confronted by a throng of people stood next to a stationary train at platform one.

We could see people clambering on the track trying to get under the front of the train. You just have to be brutal sometimes.

"Get off the tracks! Wait until we get the power off", I shouted in the general direction of those helpful members of the public, busy trying to kill themselves.

"Whisky Alpha, can we get the power off at Battersea Park Road Station and give me the confirmation when it's been done, 902 over."

"Received, will let you know immediately, Whisky Alpha, over.

"Can I have a situation report, over?" came from you know who!

We just ignored that while we got the line clear of people and I then concentrated on the driver, to see if he could reverse the train.

He wasn't too badly shaken and reversed the train about 20 metres.

My operator got some tape and cordoned off the platform as best he could. It was still impossible to keep all the 'rubberneckers' back. No matter the horror, there are always some who want to gawp and stare and generally get in the way. In the end I christened these people 'Disaster Groupies'.

"Whisky Alpha, can we have an ambulance, Scenes of Crime photographer, CID and the Duty Officer, over

"Received, I take it, it's the worst?" the expertly subtle controller kept it professional.

"Yes, we also have the lad's mate, who is telling us what happened, over.

"Received. Guvnor, did you receive the last from Whisky One, over".

"Yes, on my way there now". At least he had the decency to shut up about the bloody situation report.

We kept the driver in the cab and the public back from the edge of the platform.

The young lad on the platform was shivering, so I draped my coat over his narrow shoulders.

The sight on the tracks was grim. You look, then look away quickly. You see what you see in glimpses. Clearly a young male of about ten years, the majority of the body intact. Then you catch sight of a single white Nike trainer further down the line, with his little foot still inside.

I think the ambulance got there first, then the Duty Officer. We all waited for confirmation of the power being shut off. When it came, Scenes of Crime had got there and took as many photos as they thought necessary, then the ambulance crew had the unpleasant task of collecting the body.

By this time, with the permission of the Duty Officer, I had scooped up the victim's shivering mate and elected to take him home to his mum. The ambulance crew were wary of releasing him, but we all thought he needed his mum rather than a hospital waiting room.

He lived in one of the old Victorian terraces nearby, just around the corner. After having dropped him, I was to meet the Duty Officer at the address of the victim, where we had the awful duty to tell his next of kin.

"What's your mum's name, Darren?" I asked the lad as he sat in the back of our police car.

"Trish. Am I in trouble?".

"Let's talk to your mum first, make sure she knows you are ok?"

As we parked outside his house another lady was shouting at the occupant of his home from the front gate.

Without working it back, it was clear that this was the young victim's mum and she had found out what had happened. It can sometimes happen. Maybe someone at the railway station knew the lad. Maybe there were other kids playing this foolish game too and they'd told her or told someone who had told her. Either way I had to try and delicately get the young boy out of my car and into his house and minimise the amount of abuse he was about to get from the bereaved mum.

I took the lad while my operator had to physically hold the victim's mum back as she swore and cussed at the lad I was now virtually carrying inside his home. I said to his mum we would return and then the pair of us forced the struggling victim's mum into our car and back to her address. Once we got her inside her house, we just let her vent.

It took twenty minutes of violence, anger, blame and wailing, mostly aimed at us, before she finally subsided into a chair and lit a cigarette. My mate put the kettle on and we all sat with a tea in her living room. She stared straight ahead through her bloodshot, watering eyes and began to talk to us.

Her lad was called Tom and he was her only child. She was recently separated from his dad and she only had her mum, who lived off Eversleigh Road somewhere. My colleague discretely radioed to get a car round there to bring the grandmother down to us. We stayed as long as we could. Our Duty Officer appeared, but even he could see he was surplus to requirements and we had inadvertently done his job for him anyway. We stayed until grandma had arrived, then quietly let ourselves out and returned briefly to the other address. We told Darren's mum he might need to see a doctor and that was pretty much it. I remember we came out of that little terraced house, got back in the car and just sat there for a good ten minutes, no words, just sat with our own thoughts. Then it was back to the station for some note writing.

By this stage of my service, dealing with 'railway' incidents had become all too frequent.

On Monday 12th December 1988 just before 6am, D Relief were dismissed after a long week of Night Duty. It was always nice to get away early on the Monday morning at the end of Nights, to maximise the sleep you can get before returning for the 2pm Late shift. At this point in my career, I was just at the end of my two-year probation and I was living in my recently purchased flat in Mitcham. I was back in bed asleep by 7am. When I woke at about 12.30pm, I got myself ready for work and headed back to the station to be there for the 2pm Late Turn parade.

While I had been sleeping, a major railway incident had occurred right in the middle of our ground near to Clapham Junction Station. The Clapham rail crash.

The driver of the early morning Basingstoke to Waterloo train, made up of twelve packed commuter carriages was unable to stop when a signal changed from green to red too close to him, so he stopped at the next signal, got out and using a trackside telephone told the signal box what had happened. He was told there was no fault with the signals. Shortly after that the following train, which was another early morning packed twelve carriage commuter express from Bournemouth ploughed into the back of the stationary Basingstoke train. As this happened a train on the next line over, travelling in the opposite direction, hit the wreckage of the other trains.

The site of this happened in a steep cutting, where there is a very severe embankment and a brick wall down to the track. It made reaching the occupants of the train extremely difficult and a major incident between all the emergency services got underway.

By the time I got into work, the whole of B Relief, a newly started Street Duties course and just about everyone who could put a uniform together was down at the scene dealing with the crash. It was the Street Duties Officers first day at work since finishing their training at Hendon. You talk about a baptism of fire, these officers having to deal with the Clapham rail crash as their first ever day of duty as a police officer!

When we arrived at work, our initial role was to deal with any other calls on the ground, but also to be prepared to relieve the Early Turn. B Relief had only finished work at 10pm the previous evening and were back in relieving us at 6am, so a quick change-over themselves! Then they have a critical major incident thrown at them.

The crash happened very close to the South Circular. Spencer Park, a small green area surrounded by roads, provided an ideal and natural RVP (rendezvous point) and incident HQ. After having been on duty for less than an hour I was collected with several other foot patrol units and taken to the RVP. Not knowing what to expect we waited for our Sergeant to brief us.

One of the things about the police at a major incident is that after the initial arrival and assessment of the situation, the fire brigade and ambulance service take over. You can do little more than assist them, as they need you to facilitate their actions and requirements.

One of the requirements on this day was to help the ambulance crews and especially the mortuary attendants and pathologist to organise the bodies, prior to their relocation to the hospital mortuary. At that time next to The Roundhouse pub was a United Services and Services Rendered Club, which had offered its premises to be used as a temporary mortuary.

I said earlier that there are things that you see during your life that you cannot forget. One of these 'life's snapshots' I have, is walking into the main hall of the club to see the entire floor space filled with the bodies of those who perished in the crash. Donning gloves, I assisted in searching the clothing to reveal identities and other information about who these people were. I was there to relieve a B Relief officer who had been there from the start. I was only there for about an hour, long enough for me.

It was another numb day at work. I was tired from the changeover of shifts, so I was almost working on autopilot anyway. I did little more than support the B Relief officers and fill in wherever and whenever they needed a break. A few months later a picture was taken of Sir Peter Imbert, the Commissioner, with those B Relief and the brand-new Street Duties officers, who were the first on scene at the Clapham rail crash. That picture went up in the canteen, a daily reminder of the excellent and stoic professionalism that police officers have.

B Relief were having their share of major incidents at that time. About two weeks after the Clapham rail crash on 22nd December 1988 an IRA bomb factory was discovered on their watch in flats off Northcote Road. This discovery happened by accident. A small IRA cell had one of their number asleep in their car, parked in Bolingbroke Grove. The idea being that if they were rumbled, they would be able to get away from the scene very quickly. Or was it that one of them had had a skin full and was sleeping it off in the car?

The accidental discovery of the bomb factory was due to a local prolific motor vehicle thief, trying his luck in Bolingbroke Grove. As he moved slowly down the street trying door handles, he had no idea that anyone might actually be in one of the cars. He then tried his last door handle for that evening. Waking the IRA terrorist in the car, who, fearing that he and his colleagues have been discovered, shot the young car thief in the stomach. He ran back to the flat to alert his colleagues and they all escaped before the police arrived on the scene. What they left in their flat was a huge quantity of Semtex and other bomb making materials. The young car thief recovered from his injury and I don't believe he was ever charged with any offences.

I remain very good friends with one of the officers on duty for both the rail crash and the bomb factory incidents and asked him what it was like.

He said that everyone on his Relief wondered what was going to happen next. They had been two of the busiest weeks of his service. He was asleep on his feet from the hours he had put in. I didn't really consider it at the time, but he also had three young children at home. Now that's resilience! He added that despite their new Inspector on his Relief being a really nice bloke, they did all wonder if he was also the biggest 'Jonah' in history.

The railway could sometimes be useful too. A call came through to Battersea Station from our colleagues at Croydon one Saturday night. It was a longshot for them but they needed us to get to Clapham Junction on the hurry up to try and stop a train. There had been a serious assault and criminal damage in Croydon High Street. The suspects had decamped to East Croydon Train Station and were seen to run down the ramp to platform one, which is the platform for Victoria. The suspects were described as a group of twelve to fifteen white lads in their teens. They were all skinheads wearing tight jeans, Harrington jackets and Doc Martens boots.

The Controller at Croydon contacted Battersea by telephone direct and also put a message out via Scotland Yard over the Mains set radios in vehicles. If they had got on the next train at platform one at East Croydon, then it was bound for Victoria, only stopping at Clapham Junction. His hope was that officers could be waiting at the platform at Clapham Junction when the train pulled in and the suspects, if on board, could be detained, arrested and dealt with.

Every available unit made their way to Clapham Junction and up on to platform twelve, which we were reliably informed was where the train would come in. We had about twenty officers spread along the platform and within five minutes the train pulled in.

It was probably 10.30 – 11pm at night so the train was virtually empty. Except in carriage eight where there just so happened to be a group of sixteen skinheads in their uniform of tight jeans, Harrington jackets and DMs.

I had come up from the police station in the back of Whisky One, driven by my colleague who had given me my introduction to the delights of the Area Car. He took the lead and boarded the train, which was being held by the driver, while we sorted this out. He calmly walked up to the group spread over three or four sets of seats.

"Hello lads. Have you just come up from Croydon?"

No reply.

"Well, I think you have and there have been reports of a serious assault and criminal damage committed by a group of skinheads who match your description. You are all nicked".

I expected at this point for there to be a fairly serious 'ding-dong' with these lads but they hardly said a word. They looked fairly sheepish and also a little scared.

They were all taken off the train in handcuffs and the train was allowed to continue up to Victoria.

We handcuffed them to each other in two groups of eight and put them in the back of two vans. Wandsworth's van had very kindly got in on the act and turned up to assist.

As the offence had happened in Croydon it seemed logical for the investigation to take place there. When we arrived at Croydon Custody Suite, the Custody Sergeant had to book in our sixteen prisoners. All we had to do was complete some brief arrest notes and hand them to the Night Duty Croydon CID Officer. It looked like he might have to stay awake for the next few hours at least!

Christmas Bereavement

A Christmas Day Late shift is underway.
There is a cold, fresh breeze, and even a little sleet.
It's Fire Brigade policing on double pay.
The Relief prepare a meal. It's in the canteen we meet.

We all took turns to answer and deal with the calls.
There was nothing for me to do before refs.
I know my place, clear down and clean the plates piled tall.
There is genuine praise for our in-house chefs.

I get a message to go and speak to the controller.
I have a job allocated and head out to an address.
Other units were committed, that's why it was given to a foot patroller.
It's left to me. It's a mess.

I put on my coat and walk out to this local resident.
I try and clear my head and think about this difficult job.
"Your son was killed earlier today in a vehicle accident".
I knock at the door. A lady opens it and begins to sob.

I was invited in by this silver haired couple.
I'm not sure they understand my words, but they stoically sit.
I try and remain professional, but I know inside I'm in trouble.
Today was Christmas Day; but I'd long forgotten about it.

Christmas on the Relief in my first few years was a wonderful time. I think it had a good deal to do with the very real friendships and camaraderie that existed on D Relief. Couple that, with the fact that in the late 1980's nothing was open on Christmas Day and very little was open on Boxing Day. Even the public houses could only open for two hours at lunch time on Christmas Day. It meant that people didn't go anywhere and were content to stay at home. Most people had already travelled to be with family by Christmas Eve and there was a much smaller number of cars on the roads over the actual festive period. We did get slightly busier on Boxing Day, once families realised why they didn't see more of each other and the 'domestic' incidents started to come in.

But for those first few Christmas Days in 'The Job' we were there just in case. We didn't go out on patrol and if a call came in, we genuinely took it in turns to go out and deal with them. We were on our own at the station, just the Relief, no management or civilian support staff. Due to the numbers on the Relief, those that wanted the day off would usually be granted leave and the rest of us would scoop up the double time on offer for working a Bank Holiday.

By the time Christmas arrived on my first year with the Relief I had already cooked a couple of meals on Night Duty for the team, so it was a natural progression to offer to cook a dinner for colleagues. If you add in the Custody Sergeant, control room staff, the Late Turn CID officer and the rest of us, I cooked a dinner for about twenty people that first Late Turn Christmas.

I had a radio next to my cooking area and it was dead. The general public are content to stay at home and not seek the assistance of emergency services and clog up hospital accident and emergency departments if they have nowhere to go. The limited terrestrial television at that time would still pull out all the stops to provide extra special films and programs, because they knew that had a potential audience of twenty-plus million, all tuning in after the Queen had done her bit. I do wonder if things should have stayed like that? Do we really need shops and services to be open over the Christmas period and on Sundays? Anyway, I digress.

There was a general feeling of goodwill as we all sat down at the canteen tables, arranged so that we sat in a large square together. There may even have been crackers and paper hats. All the time there was still a listening watch going on in case someone out there needed our services. Some good banter was to be had and we were able to give our soon to be departing Inspector a few gifts and words, before his replacement (Sit. Rep.) arrived in the January.

We would get the appropriately cold, dry weather at Christmas time in those days, a hint of snow or sleet at the very least. By the time the meal was over and everything had been cleared down and cleaned away, most of us were pretty bored and simply waiting for the shift to end. I still lived in the Section House, so I wasn't really fussed either way. I was going back to my small empty room, watch a bit of television and get ready for another Late shift on Boxing Day. But Christmas Day wasn't finished yet.

Not all our Relief Christmas Days were as quiet as that first one I experienced. One year we were posted Early Turn and as I rode my trusty motorbike into the yard, shivering under my inappropriate duffle coat, there was a buzz of activity and hustle, not normally associated with Jesus' birthday. I got into the locker room and changed into my uniform and then up to the Collators office for our parade and briefing.

Half the Relief were missing. Most of the drivers and those who had got in early had gone straight out to deal with a shooting at an address at the bottom end of our ground. This was a small residential street that was at the back of Lavender Hill. It was actually next to the street where I had chased the burglar from the off licence break in on Nights some months before.

The Detective Inspector, looking more than a little pissed off, joined our Duty Officer at the parade for the rest of us. He explained that there had been a shooting and police been called to an address at around 4.30am. Night Duty units had attended and found a family in some distress, as one of the sons was clearly dead in a chair, with a gunshot wound to his head. There was mum, dad and one brother, who were all now with relatives who lived locally.

Our Early Turn units had gone up to the address to relieve the Night Duty lads, so they could get home for their own Christmas Day. Our authorised Firearms Officer (AFO) had also gone to make the weapon safe. It was common to have an AFO on Division in those days and our chap was ex-military. I forget which regiment he had been in, but other army types at Battersea had christened him 'Blanket Stacker' or simply 'Stacker', so I would suggest he wasn't infantry.

When he returned from his task and joined us for a cup of tea in the canteen, he was able to give us all a little more information. Who was the victim? Did we know him?

Well; yes, it would seem that we did…..

A little over a year earlier, the Relief was on a Saturday Night Duty shift. We dealt with the usual late evening collection of drunk drivers and some pub related disorder before things quietened down a bit and we returned to have our customary group bag of chips in the canteen. While the majority of the Relief was in munching, a call was received of a serious disturbance at a party on the 17th Floor of Totteridge House. This was a tower block of residential flats not too far from the station.

Because we were all in at the station, the vehicles were loaded up and a convoy of cars and vans screamed off down to Yelverton Road and the entrance to the tower block. Our Duty Officer was in the convoy too, so he could get his situation report in real time. We charged into the block and then stood waiting for a lift to return to the ground floor. About ten of us charged into the lift, including the boss and someone pressed 17.

I remember thinking it was like a scene near the end of the Blues Brothers film. Jake and Elwood have been chased across Illinois to Chicago by hundreds of police cars. They get to a lift and just stand quietly inside, while soothing lift music plays. That was like us, ascending to the 'ding-dong'! which was getting steadily louder as we got closer. Instead of soothing music we had our Duty Officer telling us to stay in pairs, identify and witness any potential arrests for future evidence. He was just finishing his lift briefing as the doors opened. We charged past him into the corridor, sticks draw and just got stuck into the fight. There were some who stopped fighting when we arrived and some who either carried on with each other or turned their attention to us. We got stuck into those still wanting to scrap and dragged a few down the stairs (that took a while) and ended up with a mixed bag of about six male and females under arrest. Then one of the girls kicked my reporting skipper in the bollocks, as she was being put in the van and it was all off again both inside and at the rear of the van. We got them cuffed and back to the station, eventually.

Once the dust had settled it was decided to go with a charge of Violent Disorder and they were bailed. The disturbance had started when a couple of brothers had turned up uninvited and caused problems. One of them was the former boyfriend of a girl at the party. A typical 'all over nothing' sort of fight. I remembered thinking how distinctive the surnames of the two brothers were, as they had been amongst those arrested. They had previous convictions for burglary, robbery and were known to us for possession with intent to supply drugs, possession and access to firearms. In short, a couple of wrongun's. We bailed them to their address, down on the edge of our ground, near Lavender Hill.

Six to eight months later the whole Relief trooped down to Kingston Crown Court for the trial of this violent disorder. I think it was heard at the Sessions House. The transformation of the six defendants was staggering. They were all suited and booted, the girls had slapped on some make up and the jury must have thought that butter wouldn't melt. It was painted like the entire fracas was exacerbated by the arrival of Plod and the jury came back with a Not Guilty verdict.

Initially disappointing, especially for my reporting Sergeant and his swollen Nads! The compensation was that we had virtually the entire Relief off duty in Kingston and went out for a monumental curry and several beers. I would also suggest that most of us had earned some overtime that day, as the Court date was almost certainly a rerostered rest day. The brothers may have won that round. But you never forget a name….

"Come on 'Stacker' tell us"? as we settled into an early Christmas Day brew.

These same two brothers had been at their home, most likely with a few others, but that was never proved. They had been out having a Christmas Eve drink and were back home for a night cap. The elder brother produced a nickel-plated automatic pistol and began showing it around and knowing the dick that he is / was, showing off with it! I think it may have been that he was twirling it with his finger inside the trigger guard and as the pistol's business end swung around to his head it went off. Boom! The entry wound was just to the side of one of his eyes, above the bridge of his nose. It killed him instantly.

Round two to us then. Let's call it a draw!

Back to my first Christmas Day. After our refs we were just waiting for the shift to end. I went into the control room at precisely the moment they received a telex message from Kent Constabulary. At that moment our Duty Officer and Section Sergeant were over at Wandsworth, sharing the compliments of the season with their counterparts there. The Controller looked at me and asked if I had ever delivered a 'death message' before. I hadn't, so he was dubious about sending me, but I said I was ok to go and do it. I took a note of all the details, including phone numbers and contact names down in Kent and as I left his domain he thanked me. I opened the back door of the station, that leads to the yard and felt that it was quite cold now. I went back inside and downstairs and put on my quilted car coat with the silver buttons (the Governor was at Wandsworth, so I might as well be warm).

I walked slowly down Battersea Bridge Road and into Prince of Wales Drive. It was eerily quiet, no traffic, just me pacing along, now accustomed to walking with my gloved hands clasped behind my back as I walked. The address was behind St. Marys Church, in a side road off Queenstown Road. The wind whipped down Prince of Wales Drive, making me wish I'd taken a scarf. All the time I was walking I was trying to think of the right words. Everyone in the control room had weighed in with their opinion. Be bold, be direct, be obvious. Get the message across and then temper what you say next by the bereaved couple's reaction.

The houses in Queenstown Road are former large Victorian houses of three or four storeys. Many of these had been converted into flats. The area around and behind the Church contained smaller terraced houses. Before I got to the address I contacted the control room and explained that I had arrived and would take the battery out of my radio while I was letting the parents know their son had been killed. I knocked on the black door of one of the small, terraced houses at about 7.30 in the evening. A middle-aged lady, probably mid-fifties with greying brown hair and a warm looking Christmas sweater came to the door and opened it slowly. I could see a man of similar age, slightly taller standing behind her.

"Good evening, may I come in please?" As the lady opened the door fully to allow me to enter I could see she was already weeping, a tear fell down her cheek on to her warm sweater. I walked into their small home. I could see the remains of a Christmas lunch piled up in the kitchen as they led me into their cosy lounge. I sat down opposite them, as they clasped each other's hands on their sofa.

"Is it David?" The man had second guessed me and asked about his son.

Taking the advice, I had so recently been given I just told them.

"I am so sorry to have to tell you that your son David was killed in a road traffic accident earlier this afternoon".

I stopped there, not wanting to overload them with information. That could come after the initial impact of what I had said sank in.

But they were incredible. They were completely devastated for me to have to be the bearer of such awful news. I was given a cup of tea and they asked how my Christmas Day had been.

I realise they were in shock and I am not sure they had taken in such horrific news. I saw a notepad on the table and jotted down as much information as I had about the incident, who was a point of contact in Kent, who they could reach out to.

I stayed with that poor couple for over an hour. I was shown pictures of their son David on the day of his graduation from university. They told me about how he had been with his girlfriend last night in Tunbridge Wells and was coming to see them that evening. It was heart breaking and gut wrenching to listen to, but that's all I did, just listened.

I think they noticed how affected by all this I was and it was them they said that I ought to be going. They once again thanked me for telling them and said they would contact the Kent officer in due course. They wished me well and to stay safe as they showed me to the door. This had been the first 'death message' I had ever given. It was incredibly hard. Over the years I delivered many such messages. It never got any easier. Peoples' reactions were always different, but none were ever as empathetic to my situation as the quiet couple in that small, terraced house near to Queenstown Road on Christmas Day.

As I came out of the address I could see the Area Car was parked up just down the street. Without being asked they had just turned up and waited for me to finish with the job. They were there to give me a lift back to the station.

"Nice coat! Better change out of that before the Guvnor sees you", and we laughed as I got in the back.

While Christmas Day was often a very quiet shift, Boxing Day could usually be relied upon to be anything but.

Some years after my first Christmas and I was posted driving Whisky One, Early Turn on Boxing Day. As was usually the case, all the crews got in early when posted to the Area Car and we made a special effort to get in early this Boxing Day, so the Night

Duty crew I was relieving could get home quickly. Normally on any Early Turn there would be time for a brew and a bit of a chat in the canteen, before taking the car out and even more so on a Bank Holiday. But not on this morning.

The Night Duty controller spoke to us about a situation they had at an address up near the junction with Bolingbroke Grove. This was right at the bottom end of our ground, near to where Tooting Division would patrol. A male was barricaded in his house with his teenage daughter and the wife feared for her safety. Apparently, a massive domestic row had turned ugly and physical, resulting in the wife being assaulted with a kitchen knife and the husband grabbing his daughter and sealing himself in the front room. There were several Night Duty units down there and the controller wanted me to go down and relieve some of them, until the rest of my Relief turned up for work.

We got down to the address and were brought up to speed by our colleagues there. They had been chatting with the male for about an hour. It was a row that had started over their daughter and her behaviour. The man and woman were known to us for domestic violence and on an alcohol fuelled Christmas Day, it had eventually (and inevitably) gone pear-shaped. He had slashed his wife with a small kitchen knife, then grabbed the daughter and gone into the front room and thrown furniture against the doors. It was believed he still had the knife. Officers could see the man through the back window and were talking to him through the lounge door closest to the front of the house. There was a second door further down the hallway and a third door at the back of the front room, that led to the kitchen.

"Have you got any riot gear in the back?" the van driver asked.

In the boot I had a couple of short shields, two NATO helmets and a selection of knee and elbow protectors. These were the days before the introduction of ASP's (gravity friction lock batons) or Tasers. We were packing the long black acrylic batons at that stage.

A plan was hatched to distract the man, so we could get the girl out of the lounge and then confront the male, detain and arrest him. While I and another officer picked up a shield each, put on the protectors and helmets the other officers tried to talk the man back towards the front of the room. As they did so, at a given signal, two officers would put in the kitchen door and grab the daughter. Simultaneously we would put in the front lounge door and subdue the male. Best laid plans.

"Go!"

Great signal. We crashed through the door, pretty much destroying it and the coffee table that he had upended against it. As we entered he was in the middle of the room, with his back to us, watching as his daughter was grabbed by other officers and dragged into the kitchen.

"Drop the knife, stand still and put your hands in the air", my mate bellowed.

He turned towards us and didn't do any of that. He moved towards me, with the knife in his right hand. As he lunged forward I hit him using the short shield with as much force as I could muster as I swayed to the right. I managed to hit him on the side of his shoulder. He fell to his right and into the path of my mates shield that hit him full in the face. Down he went, blood pouring from his nose, knife dropped, on to his front and hand cuffed. The Night Duty units were not too late off and Whisky One had one in the bin before 6am.

The wife had a slash wound to her upper arm that needed a dozen stitches and thankfully the daughter was unharmed. The male had a broken nose and had lost a tooth and was

charged with something pathetic like Actual Bodily Harm which never went anywhere, because the wife dropped it all when they got back together by New Year.

Mortuary and a Jolly Jape!

A Street Duties visit to witness a postmortem
The 'Old Sweat' tutor had his wind up in mind.
His way to lower anxiety levels in them
It had become a frequent right of passage; but was it kind?

Unknown to him a cunning plan was put in motion.
Pre-empt this routine and catch him at his own game.
A fellow tutor, about to leave following promotion,
Arrived early. Perhaps frighten him too, was his aim.

He secreted himself on a shelf in the cold store,
A white sheet covering his uniformed shape.
The main tutor arrived and took up position, as he'd done before.
The mortuary attendant assisting him in this 'jolly jape'.

There are two serving officers locked in the cooler.
The first one keeps motionless in the pitch-black space.
Noises from outside are heard, but much fainter.
One officer waiting for his cue. How I wished I'd seen the other's face.

"Cold in here; isn't it!" the first copper chuckled.
The tutor screams, "Get me out, get me out!"
The door swung open and the 'Old Sweat' is completely ruffled.
This wind up had run its course, of that there was no doubt!

You have got to love a wind up. Police officers are human. They regularly deal with the inhuman, but they are just the same as everyone and they do have a wicked and some would say warped sense of humour. This often manifests itself in jokes played upon each other. All sorts of fiendishly clever and cunning scenes and ideas are played out. Part of a rite of passage for the new and young recruits joining the Relief. Was it harsh and extreme? Was it bullying? I'm not sure it would survive the scrutiny of today's modern ultra-sensitive society, but I believe it made the person concerned feel accepted and welcome amongst the team and therefore was not harsh or oppressive.

Sometimes they were simple and basic, others involved intricate planning and cooperation from a number of different officers, neighbouring divisions and other agencies. If an individual on the Relief had a skill or unique hobby, then that could sometimes be used to assist in the wind up. Sometimes the intended target is not always the one that everyone expects it is…

The poem above described one such wheeze, where eventually the Relief decided to play it back on the tutor. It was a wind up that he had been doing with every Street Duties course he had run and one day it was decided that it might be fun to tweak the ruse, just a little. The original idea was quite simple. The Street Duties course would invariably at some stage during their ten-weeks, go to the hospital mortuary to witness a postmortem and have a question and answer session with the pathologist. It was both educational and helped cope with dealing with the dead.

The tutor had worked out with the mortuary technician an

understanding that he would be secreted in the large body sized fridges. When the mortuary attendant opened the door and pulled the platform out, the tutor would be lying there under a sheet. The sheet would be pulled back to reveal the smiling tutor, to gasps and laughter from his young charges. You can never put a finger on who came up with the scheme to sabotage this 'jolly jape', but ultimately a plan was put in place.

A senior member of the Relief got down to the hospital early and collared the technician. He knew there was a Street Duties group due in at 9am. He also knew that the senior tutor would attend at about 8.45am and get himself in position in the fridge. The man at the mortuary agreed to put the other officer on the next-door platform at about 8.30am. The first officer is in position and he waits until he hears the tutor arrive and get himself on to the sliding platform and then the fridge door is once again closed. I always think timing is everything. The first officer waits until things settle down. He said that he could hear movement outside as the young recruits arrived for their visit. That's when he spoke.

"Cold in here, isn't it?" in a calm otherworldly voice.

Screams were heard around a good section of the hospital as the technician got the tutor out of his cooler to much laughter and merriment from the Relief officer when he too, was released.

"You bastard", the tutor was laughing too.

If you were ever doing a wind up on someone, it was always a good idea to keep one eye looking over your shoulder.

We had one that was worked out using two young female officers from Wandsworth that wouldn't be known to our young officer (victim). He received a call over his radio of a couple of suspects within the confines of the secure Heliport, just off Lombard Road, down by the river. He and other units made their way and having secured all the exits, this young officer was put to work searching the area around the compound. After a short search he came across two scruffily dressed white females hiding behind some wooden pallets. He arrested the two and they were handcuffed and placed in the back of the van. He then got in the back with the two females, which in hindsight was the first point of when he might have guessed all was not right. Back at the station, out of the van and up the steps into the charge room.

"He fuckin' groped my arse", from the mouth of one of the girls.

"Yeah, and he fondled my tits", from the other.

The arresting officer was dumbstruck.

The Custody Sergeant immediately went into proper protocol and told the officer he was under arrest for the allegation of a sexual assault. He was processed, fingerprinted and photographed. The uniform he was wearing was seized and he was put into a prisoner's paper suit (but it did have his epaulettes in biro on the shoulders, which was a nice touch) and then put in a cell.

Everyone got involved. The Night Duty CID officer came and told him that he would be interviewed shortly after a full statement had been taken from the girls. The Duty Officer informed him that complaints would need to speak to him in the morning. To the officer's eternal credit, he held it together and stated.

"Can you tell my wife, get me a solicitor and book me on for overtime please."

As he walked into the interview room the two scruffy females he had arrested were by now back in their police uniforms, smiling as he came through the door. It took him a while to ping them as the two he had arrested earlier. The CID officer introduced him to two WPCs from Wandsworth, assisting in this D Relief wind up.

He stood for a moment taking it all in before with a huge grin on his face he spoke.

"You utter, utter, bastards"!

There was a very plausible telex message that had been concocted one Night Duty. It had come from one of our controllers, but it had all the authenticity of a message from The Yard. This particular wind up required the use of a parked-up wagon on one of the industrial estates that was seen to have a selection of HAZCHEM warning stickers on it. One such vehicle was found in an area close to the old Guinness Brewery site, off York Road.

The message required officers to attend and confirm the lorry and its load was there and that the load was secure and not damaged in any way. The message went on to say that the cargo could possibly contain radioactive waste and as such, officers were advised to be extremely careful. (No shit!). Somehow the two officers chosen to attend, didn't immediately see through this and made their way to the scene. During this time another officer had deposited the contents of a couple of tubs of fluorescent green slime at the corner of the cargo container, all we had to do was wait.

The two officers attended and discovered the slime. They withdrew from the container and called it in. This was where the controller earned his keep. He made it sound like he was reading from a manual. He instructed the two officers to return to the police station and wait in the yard. Due to their proximity to the cargo, it would be necessary to hose them down with fresh water in the yard. You can see where this is going.

The two officers stripped to their underpants and were hosed down pretty much by the rest of the Relief for about 10 minutes. They had been told that the nature of the cargo was so dangerous that it could possibly render them sterile, therefore they readily agreed to be hosed down with water for at least 10 minutes, as per the instructions on the ever so convincing telex message. One of the two even asked for a second dousing to be sure he was safe and that might even have been after the wind up was revealed to him, he was so concerned.

Another occasion required one of our colleagues to bring his scuba equipment into work one Night Duty. The set up was very straight forward. A probationer was called to go to Battersea Park, where a member of the public (controller) had reported a body floating near the island in the middle of the lake. A good number of the Relief were already in position with excellent vantage points of the lake. The 'body' was, as you might have guessed, the scuba expert who had his tank on his front and had donned a civilian jacket and was floating face down in the lake, as the witness (controller) had described.

The foot-patrolling probationer made his way into the park and across to the dimly lit lake area. He had been joined by one of the Section Sergeants, who was universally accepted as having the best chance of anyone in keeping a straight face. When they arrived, the probationer suggested they perhaps try and use one of the rowing boats to get out to the shape in the water. Quick as a flash the skipper says they would all be locked up at this time of night and he'll have to wade in and see if he can reach whatever it is.

The young Constable removes his trousers and slowly lowers himself into the water, radio in one hand, trying to keep it out of the water. The water comes up to just above his waist. At one stage he was trying to keep his tunic out of the water, but quickly gives that up as the water gets a little deeper and he wades out towards the island and the object floating in front of him. The officer finally reached the object, which is by now clearly a body, face down in the water. It was virtually pitch black, so it must have been both convincing and a little terrifying.

The officer reaches out and grabs the shoulder of the body. As he does so the thing rolls slowly over and Scuba boy goes "Boo"!

The officer screamed and fell back into the water, drenching the rest of himself. Simultaneously all the headlights of the hidden police vehicles come on illuminating the scene. Aquaman helped get the young officer back to the shore with much coughing and spluttering with an impressive catalogue of swear words too!

"You fucking bastards!", he was smiling as he squelched into the back of the van.

The time I was called to go to Battersea Park myself.

"902, can you attend the main football pitches in the park at 3pm. India 99 (police helicopter) is landing with a VIP and they need an officer on the ground, Whisky Alpha, over"

"Received, on my way, 902, over".

I made my way, completely unsuspecting of anything, to the location and called up to say that I had arrived. I was actually a little excited that I might get to see a mildly famous celebrity.

"902, wait one. We are just going to patch you through to India 99 direct, Whisky Alpha, over".

"Received, 902, over".

I quite legitimately now believed I would be in direct communication with the police helicopter as it came to land in the middle of the Battersea Park football pitches.

In reality, the Controller at Battersea had a colleague stood behind him and on every purported transmission from the helicopter, the colleague was beating his fist on his chest to simulate helicopter rotors.

Well it sounded convincing enough to me. Enough for me to follow the helicopters instructions to wave my arms in the air, jump up and down, spin around and do star jumps. All of these calisthenics in full view of the surreptitiously parked collection of 'mates' on the Relief.

About 10 minutes of this before the penny dropped and I swore I could hear giggling on the radio channel.

"Bastards!"

There were so many more than to commit to the page here. Coppers when they are called to, work incredibly hard and are brave and supportive. They also have a cunning and devious wit, coupled with imagination. I never, at any stage, felt I was being picked on or singled out for any of the wind ups played on me. Society and perhaps sensibilities were different then. I never felt bullied, in fact quite the contrary. It made me feel part of the team, an accepted colleague and someone who could be trusted.

In a job where at any moment you have to deal with something dreadful, or put yourself in harm's way, you need to have a balance, a lighter side. I always thought of wind ups as part of the bonding process.

Aid Opportunities

You have a choice. Drive the Carrier for Notting Hill.
Or five days at The Oval test match versus The Windies?
Tricky One. Guess I'll head to Kennington Oval and chill.
A smile from the Duties Sergeant. He always tried to please.

The first two days were re-rostered rest days.
I remember on the Saturday a fabulous Lara century.
Absolutely no trouble in the crowd. How well he plays.
I took position opposite the Pavilion, on a cushion, lent to me.

The main thing on Sunday, apart from our reassuring presence.
Was to ensure we all turned out on Bank Holiday Monday.
A hope that the game went the full distance.
All down to England's batting, let us pray.

A fortuitously slow game. Mr. Lara excepted.
Ensured we all paraded for day five, double time.
A briefing declared streakers were expected.
But the Oval employed runners, so not our crime.

Almost a week of blissful, trouble-free aid.
An oasis of time and a welcome tour of duty.
Oh, for cricket every week, so at The Oval I could have stayed.
Don't forget to bring a bottle, for the Duty Sergeant's booty!

Aid, the chance for the Duties to completely fuck up your weekend and any social life. On most weekends, a number of officers from Borough policing duties would be required to be taken, en masse, to assist in policing some event in another part of town. It might be a football match, demonstration or another occasion requiring extra police. All aid was a pain, but over the years I got used to it and ensured it worked for me!

By 1995, I had been on uniform Beat Duty at Battersea for almost ten years. Things had started to change about how we were expected to police the streets. I sensed that my time at Battersea was coming to an end and I was looking to make that change on my terms, rather than have it forced upon me. Then, in the midst of all these difficult decisions and uneasy feelings, the Duties Sergeant made me a short-term offer I couldn't refuse.

It was that time of year once again. Notting Hill was approaching and there was every possibility I would not be able to get out of it this year. I had avoided it for a few years, but sometimes you are just in the cross hairs of life and I could see Notting Hill being squarely aimed my way!

I ambled into the Duties Office on the first floor to be greeted by the Duties Sergeant, a recently appointed beast of a man, with a head the size of a buffalo! He had an interesting choice to offer me for the August Bank Holiday weekend. He needed a couple of level two trained carrier drivers. One required to drive a serial to Notting Hill for the two days of the carnival and one to drive a serial to Kennington Oval cricket ground to cover the up-coming test match between England and the West Indies.

What a tricky choice! I mulled this over for a fraction of a second before choosing the test match. That was that. I would not be going to Notting Hill, but instead would spend five days at the England versus West Indies cricket match at Kennington Oval. Although I didn't know it at the time, this was in fact the last sporting aid that I ever did.

Aid up town could be deathly boring, but just occasionally, something would happen. You knew it was going to be a long day if the first thing that happened was you all got fed at the vast feeding centre at Buckingham Gate. It was also sometimes a serious security event, like for example the G7 conference in 1991. The leaders of seven of the most advanced economies in the world at that time, with the addition of the Russian leader, Mikhail Gorbachev, invited as a guest. All of our supervisors disappeared for an upstairs briefing, while we ate and someone grabbed our box of snacks.

When our Inspector and Sergeants returned to our table they were carrying several sheets of paper and briefed us on our role that day. One of the events was a speech to be delivered by Mikhail Gorbachev at the Queen Elizabeth Conference Centre, which sits almost opposite Westminster Abbey, just by Parliament Square. A very public and prominent area of London and very much in the full glare of the world's media. Our duty was to patrol in pairs around the environs of the conference centre, including the side roads behind and into Parliament square. It was another duty without our own radios, just the supervisors were in communication with the Commanders.

During the extended briefing we were each given the papers the supervisors had been holding. They contained pictures of a selection of individuals likely to turn up to these events, with a possibility of them causing trouble or worse, being a known threat and danger to those present. It was a typical hand out for such a day, with the quality of the photocopied pictures fairly poor.

You always have a brief glance at these pictures, then usually put them in a pocket in your uniform somewhere, to be forgotten until your kit needs dry cleaning months later. As I said, the quality of the pictures is poor and you never really believe that real people actually look like this. The Sergeant who handed the pictures out to us mentioned that on the second page there was a chap who was a known activist, known from past events across Europe to be a 'stalker' of the Russian leader, Mikhail Gorbachev. Intelligence believed him to be in the UK, with a very real possibility that he would show up and could pose a threat to Gorbachev.

We were given about twenty minutes to be ground assigned and we walked from the feeding centre down to Victoria Street and then up towards Parliament Square and the area we were to patrol. It's a busy part of London, more so on this day due to this world event taking place. We began our patrol in pairs, doing a circuit of the area and getting occasional updates from our Sergeant as he met us.

I think expectation within the public had risen with our increased presence and a crowd formed behind some barriers running along Victoria Street, in front of our position. A short distance from my position I saw a man with a rucksack begin to climb a lamp post.

My colleague and I walked to the foot of the lamp post and I told the man to climb back down. He looked down at me. I would say he was about ten feet off the ground. He ignored my command and clung to his position. My colleague knelt down and I got on his shoulders, me being somewhat lighter. He then rose to his feet and I managed to grab the lamp post monkey's ankles and with a firm pull I was able to return him to the pavement, where he lay on his back, a bit like an overturned crab, struggling to right itself.

Back on terra firma myself we hauled the chap to his feet. By now the Sergeant had returned and he called the Command for the day and asked for a van for a prisoner. I'd nicked him for something like Highway Obstruction or Breach of the Peace. It was as I searched him on the street I actually looked at him closely. I pulled out my paper handout of photographs and flicked to the Gorbachev stalker. My arrest was him, without doubt, despite the poor quality of the print, it was the same person.

My Skipper concurred and we waited for a van to arrive. About five minutes later a local van appeared and my colleague and I put our prisoner in the back and got in. We got to the Custody Suite at Bow Street. I gave my evidence of arrest to the Sergeant. I also brought to his attention the likeness of this chap to the photograph of Gorbachev's stalker. Our man was not talking English either. He studied the image and then the prisoner and nodded sagely at us both. He was put in a cell and we went off to find somewhere to write our notes. Within about ten minutes two very smartly dressed men in their thirties walked into the interview room where we were busy writing.

'Good morning officers, I understand that you have possibly detained someone who may be of interest?'

"Err! Well, err, yes. We think he may be the person who has been stalking Mr. Gorbachev", I failed to ask who these very well-spoken men were, as I answered, but put that down to my lack of experience and the politeness shown to us by these two suited gentlemen.

"Excellent; we can take it from here. If you just hand me your notes, you can return to your patrol", one of them reached down and picked up our unfinished Incident report books.

With this, they then departed, leaving us sitting, somewhat stunned in the small interview room. After a short while we got our kit together and decided to walk back to the location of our security patrol. The rest of the day passed off without incident and we were eventually dismissed and returned to Battersea.

I had forgotten the whole thing by the time a note appeared in my correspondence tray months later, requesting that I go and see the Superintendent the following day. This usually meant that I had done something wrong or was in trouble again. I attended at the appointed time and sat down opposite my senior officer. He smiled and stated that it was nice to be sitting down with me to discuss such a positive matter, a welcome change!

The two gentlemen at Bow Street Police Station had turned out to be Special Branch Officers, who had attended to take over the investigation of our lamp post climbing stalker. A letter had been received by my Superintendent from his opposite number at Special Branch complimenting me for my diligence and excellent work at the G7 conference. Though they were not at liberty to go into detail, the arrest had been an important one for the safety of several VIP guests to these shores and also a good deal of useful intelligence had been obtained.

My boss stated that although no formal commendation could be given for the work, that he would ensure that the letter would be placed on my file, as a record of my efforts while policing the G7 Conference.

I always studied any hand outs and photographs at future events and explained why to my junior colleagues. It may be bollocks most of the time, but on occasion………you just never know!

The first few years of my service we used to get bussed across the river on most Saturdays to police the Chelsea football game. Stamford Bridge was a very different place back in the 1980's. I only stood in The Shed end of the ground once. The home of the local supporters. You would never stand at the front. If you did, the fans directly behind you would urinate on you and I have already stated how useless the raincoat was. We would also police Crystal Palace games, once they got promoted. Very occasionally I might have to do QPR or something tasty like West Ham versus Millwall. That was always a busy day!

Not being a devoted fan of football, I could take it or leave it. Some colleagues really liked football and would volunteer to do most games. I always felt that was a bit of a gamble. We were being driven in and there was every possibility that W Division would be given some God forsaken traffic deployment nowhere near the game anyway. The sporting stuff I was always keen to get involved with was the Rugby at Twickenham. The Five Nations Championship, as it then was and the recently implemented Rugby World Cup.

My first ever aid to a sporting fixture was down to Twickenham. We were put on a bus at Battersea, which had already picked up Wandsworth and Tooting colleagues. Off we went for a day out Policing the Middlesex Sevens rugby tournament. Like Stamford Bridge, Twickenham was a very different stadium to the one that exists today, too. Three sides of it were these old green roofed terraces, with a more modern South Stand, which stood alone. Behind the West Stand was a very large car park, where patrons could leave their cars and walk into the ground. We were given a briefing by the Twickenham officer in charge. We were to keep a low profile and ensure the safety of the crowd. The extended nature of the Sevens tournament that day, would mean a very long tour of duty for all concerned. This might well result in an over-indulgence in alcohol! I always presumed that he meant the crowd, but as the day wore on and events unfolded, maybe he was talking about everyone?

I was paired up with an older colleague from Wandsworth who I had never met before. At that stage of my service, all my colleagues were much older than me. He was extremely polite and actually spoke to me. We had one radio between the two of us, which he had responsibility for. Our initial task was to stand at the back of the South Stand and just keep an eye on things. For those that don't know, there is never any trouble at rugby matches. The crowds of fans mix with each other and apart from some drunken exuberance and illness, I can't think of an occasion when I had to do anything when policing rugby.

We stayed in the South Stand for about ten minutes. My colleague suggested that we meander our way out of the stadium into the West car park, where he knew that several of his friends who were attending the tournament would be. I didn't question his decision and we walked out of the ground and into the busy car park. The beauty of the Sevens matches was that it allowed fans to come and go, following the progress of their teams. Those in the West car park had got themselves very well set up. Most had food and wine spread out on the rear boot lids of their four by fours. My Wandsworth colleague found his friends behind a white, hire van. They had a barrel of lager and one of bitter set up and a table laden with French sticks, pâté, cheeses, salads and boxes of wine. They also had deck chairs forming a crescent around the rear of their van.

My colleague took some liquid refreshment and offered it to me. Was it some sort of test? Anyway, I took it and was offered a deck chair. I was also handed a fully loaded French baguette rammed with selected meats, cheeses and salad. So, there we were, two W District uniformed officers (helmets off), sat in deck chairs in the West car park of Twickenham, 'policing' the rugby. This was one of the first times I had ever done aid and it was probably one of the best days in uniform I ever had. Not that it's easy to remember the detail. I think when we sat down in those deck chairs to tuck into those French sticks and our refreshing drinks it was only about midday. Every so often my colleague would answer a radio message. I asked him what they wanted.

"Just an overview of things in the South Stand"! which he had given them from his reclining position in a deck chair, in the West car park. That afternoon was a splendid few hours spent sitting in the sun, supping several drinks. At one stage we did wander into the stadium to see how things were going. We ran into several of our W serial colleagues who all seemed to be in good spirits too. No one could find the Inspector, but the Sergeants had everything under control.

I do remember my new best friend from Wandsworth having to assist me out of the deck chair, eventually.

"Come on, we've been dismissed and we need to go back to the coach".

He was almost carrying me by the time we reached the steps of the coach. I lurched on board and made my way to a seat near the back. A Sergeant from Tooting got on board. They had provided the Inspector in charge of us that day. He did a head count and we were missing two constables and the Inspector. After about another twenty minutes, although as far as I was concerned it could have been hours, the two constables returned carrying the Inspector and somehow threw him into a seat. This sudden jolt roused him and with an unintelligible roar he exclaimed,

"Lessgo!".

What a brilliant day out. I was concerned that I would be in a world of trouble for my behaviour, but I clearly hadn't scratched the surface compared to the Tooting Inspector. He was virtually unconscious by the time we were all dropped off at Battersea. I had travelled into work that morning on my trusty motorbike and

I would suggest that if I could have found it or been able to stand unaided I might have attempted to ride it home to the Section House. Luckily one of the Late Turn Relief got me into his Panda and gave me a lift back to my digs.

On the day of the 1991 Rugby World Cup final between England and Australia, a serial was sent down from Battersea. This time we were in a carrier, but I wasn't driving. I might have been suspended from driving at that moment in time. We had a briefing and then were allocated our patrols. All of the Battersea officers were posted to a selection of traffic points, some not even within sight of the stadium. Imagine that? You are at the rugby, but not really. You are actually about half a mile away in Kneller Fucking Road, while the Rugby World Cup final is taking place within earshot.

I knew from chatting to friends in other units and the TSG, that there were off-duty serials who had drifted into the ground in uniform to watch the game.

"*Bugger this*", I thought, and two of us managed to get in to see a bit of the second half. Well until Campese's try finished England off and then we hastily ran back to our spot in Kneller Fucking Road. Still, at least we saw a bit of it. It was most often the case at Twickenham as my service wore on that we would get an outside role. In case you are not aware, it's just called Kneller Road, but to me it will always be…. Kneller Fucking Road!

I did get to do an England v Wales five nations game inside on one occasion. I still have the program from that game somewhere. I remember it mostly for the misfortune that happened to my posted partner that day. We were at the top of the South Stand again, which afforded a cracking view of the game. There were some toilets right at the back and I spied a punter staggering out of them. My 'oppo' didn't see him until it was too late. I moved out of the line of fire as he projectile vomited all over my partners shoes and trousers.

"Fucks sake"! My colleague grabbed him and frog marched him to the top of the stand, all the while this chap was puking up beer and semi-digested burger. He wasn't arrested. Two of his friends had seen what had happened and came up to us and assured my mate that they would take care of Mr. Sick. They then carried him back to the toilets to clean him up a bit, while my grumbling partner did the same. You see, never any problem at the rugby!

Another aid posting I recall was to Wembley stadium. It was rare for Battersea Division to get aid to Wembley. What made this even stranger was that it wasn't even for a sporting fixture. It was Saturday 31st August 1991, a week after the Notting Hill Carnival, which I had not been able to miss. To be honest I was completely pissed off with aid by that stage of the summer and here I was, another week and another Saturday on aid.

We got fed somewhere, I can't recall exactly where, it was probably Buckingham Gate. We were briefed by an Inspector from Wembley about what we were likely to expect from today's event. It was a rock concert by Guns N' Roses, as part of their 1991 '*Use your Illusion*' Tour. Now I have to say I'd bought their 1987 album '*Appetite for Destruction*' and liked their music, so I was more than keen to get inside the stadium and see what they were like live. But that was not on the briefing agenda from the Wembley boss.

I was posted with several other officers initially to a car park and environs patrol. Then as the punters started to arrive, we were to take up position near to a set of turnstiles to ensure public safety and prevent disorder. After a brief surge to enter the stadium when the venue opened, things calmed down a bit as the afternoon wore on. I found myself chatting to one of the marshals employed by Wembley to deal with controlling the crowds inside the ground. We were at the top of the steps, so I had a good view of the queue to get in and could also see how many of the crowd were streaming to get to the front of the pitch area for the closest view of the concert to come.

Our conversation continued and eventually he asked me if, once the concert got underway, I would like to come and see for myself. Yes please! I watched the numbers of the crowd dwindle to a trickle and walked inside with the marshal. I was able to see a good thirty to forty-five minutes of the show before returning to my allocated patrol duty. Guns N' Roses were pretty good, maybe not as good as the hype, but it was an impressive show from the back of the stadium.

At this stage of my service, I was sometimes just plain lucky or very cunning and could inveigle my way on to some cushier option. One such moment was when I was selected for the Youth Diversion scheme one summer.

Rarely, something a little different would happen. By pure chance or stars aligning, I would find myself fulfilling an altogether different role. Something fitting this category occurred towards the end of my time at Battersea.

A colleague and good friend to this day had become involved with organising the Wandsworth Borough Summer Youth Diversion Scheme. Very modern, very politically correct, very new! A multi-agency approach to finding fulfilling things to do for some of the disaffected youth of the Borough. Funded through the council and other sponsors, the idea was to occupy some of the more challenging young adults and lead them into situations and opportunities they would otherwise never contemplate.

A partnership had been forged between us up in London and the Navy, in the shape of the HMS Raleigh Naval training establishment on the outskirts of Plymouth. Carefully selected youngsters would be driven down to the Naval base to be hosted by them for a week of exhilarating activities and challenges.

At the outset, picking the candidates proved to be the first challenge. The syndicate of selectors had filled the early roster with a selection of under achieving and problematic cases, but it seemed, certainly to my colleague and I, that it would be a bit narrow to offer such a wonderful opportunity solely to miscreants and troublesome teens and we suggested balancing the final group with several high achieving cases. Our point of view was, rather surprisingly, accepted and the quota was increased with several top students and other outstanding teens. A delicate mix of young girls and boys aged between 16 and 18 years.

On a supervisory level, the selection was much simpler. My mate picked me and a female officer we both knew and Wandsworth Council chose a female from their Social Services department.

So off we went, crammed into two vans, eight teens and two supervisors to a van, me driving one and my mucker driving the other. I drew the longer straw and had the company of the female officer, while my mate had the delightful company of the social worker, who could have been carved straight from the stereotype.

As I was enjoying the drive down, with our charges lurching from hyped up excitement to bored lethargy, I was asked by one, as we passed some livestock in a field.

"What is that?"

"That, young man, is a cow!" I realised it was going to be a very long but rewarding week.

Upon arrival at HMS Raleigh we were met by our Naval liaison, Bob. He was fantastic. Boundless enthusiasm and fitter than a butcher's dog, which he proved continually during the week. A packed itinerary had been devised by him to occupy our group and the first stop was the kit store. Everyone was given a decent pair of boots, coveralls, belts, rucksacks, waterproofs, hats, gloves, torches, stoves, rations, tee shirts, shorts, socks. Everything you would need for all the exciting adventures Bob had planned for us. All the supervisors were included and we got the same kit as all the new 'recruits'.

Next stop were our billets. A dormitory for the young men and one, a reasonable distance away, for the young ladies. One supervisor to sleep in each dormitory, the other two had their own room. If memory serves we may have done half a week each in the dormitory and single rooms, to share the supervisory duties.

Everyone got changed into their new 'ad hoc' uniforms and we were escorted to the mess hall. Some of our young charges were overwhelmed by the variety and amount of food on offer and proceeded to choose a plentiful selection. But it was our young social worker who stole the show.

As we queued along the buffet style food counter, she caught the eye of a particularly large, bald-headed chap in his chef's whites.

"Do you have a vegetarian option?", she asked very politely. Now this was in about 1994 and attitudes towards the alternative dietary requirements of some had not, at that time, reached places like HMS Raleigh.

The bullet-headed chef stared for a while, then smiled, then frowned, when he realised she was serious.

"Err! I'll see what I can do, you go and sit down and I'll bring you something over", he said and disappeared into the kitchen behind the counter.

As we all sat eating our steaks, lamb chops and chicken legs, plates piled high with chips we all wandered what dish might appear for our vegetarian colleague. After about ten minutes, the ogre in the chef's rig reappeared and placed a steaming plate of pasta in a red sauce in front of her.

"There you are Miss, enjoy!" Everyone saw the smile on his face as he walked back to his kitchen.

She began to tuck in and ate a good portion of the meal before she asked for a large glass of water.

"Everything ok?' my friend in charge asked.

"It's very nice, but a bit hot and spicy for me", she smiled back.

I tasted a little, upon her invitation. HOT! I should say so! My mouth was on fire after one small mouthful.

To the chef's credit he then spent the rest of the week producing very palatable options for our lady vegetarian.

After eating, I was rather hoping to be able to just sit and have a relaxing evening. Possibly a few beers and recover from the long day getting down to Devon. However, when you have sixteen young adults in your care, rest and relaxation are never on the cards. They needed some activity to wear them out. Like taking a dog on a long walk, but it would have to be more entertaining than that.

Bob offered us use of one of the gyms and we then had to decide what activity to do. Boys wanted football, girls, less so. They wanted volleyball. Here is where my great friend showed his leadership strength and with the wisdom of Solomon, he said we could split the time and do volleyball, then football. We did just that, with the time available, evenly between the two activities.

He would be most hurt if I didn't mention that his team won the volleyball and as I write this now, I am imagining his smiling face looking down at me at the conclusion of the contest, some thirty years ago and pronouncing to these impressionable teenagers.

"Now that, Ladies and Gentlemen, is a loser"! With that he helped me to my feet and we quickly switched to football, where I sulked in goal!

Our first day had been a whirlwind of travelling and acclimatising to our new surroundings. All we had to do now was to ensure they all slept soundly. For my part, in my private room, away from the dormitories, I had a splendid and peaceful eight hours sleep and awoke ready for day two.

After a hearty breakfast, Bob had the group on parade in front of the billet at 9am. He had been joined by two of his colleagues to assist in the planned 10 mile walk up on Dartmoor.

There followed, that week, a myriad of outward bound and adventurous activities to keep our charges occupied. After all, the whole point of the exercise was to provide something for these individuals to do during the summer.

There were one or two moments, where personalities clashed and not just the youngsters! But by the time we came to the end of the week, the young women and men had begun to show a camaraderie and team spirit as they worked together to overcome the challenges that Bob, our fantastic naval liaison, placed upon them.

He was omnipresent during the week. Hiding, like a crocodile, in the reeds of the pool through which you had to wade as part of the assault course, carrying his own and at least two of the youngster's rucksacks during one of the more strenuous Dartmoor hikes. Finally, he entered us into a competitive walk across the Moor against Naval recruits. By sheer tenacity of will on his part, he got our motley collection of displaced London teenagers across the line in first place.

The final memory of the week away was the journey back in the two vans. We were persuaded by the youngsters to stop for a snack at a burger van on the A303. To be fair, everyone was hungry and the menu looked very appetising. Bacon sandwiches or rolls all round? And as for the social worker, who was looking at a particularly low ebb at that moment?

'May I have a bacon roll too, please!", she smiled. Too hungry to resist the mouth-watering smell of the frying bacon.

The Diversion scheme ran for several years. Sadly, money started to become scrutinised more and someone with no idea about youngsters made the decision that all future schemes should take place within the Metropolitan area and that was that!

Back to 1995 and the 6th test match that summer between England and the West Indies at the Kennington Oval. My own supervising skipper was in charge of our carrier for the (hopefully) five days of the match. Our role was to patrol inside the ground, primarily behind the stands to ensure public safety and deal with any incidents that might occur. My responsibility was also the security of our vehicle and to make sure it was readily available, should it be needed.

I have to say at the outset, that I love the game of cricket. Even with the advent of the fifty over format, T20, Big bashes and the Indian Premier League, I still prefer Test Match cricket. I hear people say, they can't understand how a game can go on for five days and end in a draw, but they're missing the point. It's nuanced and tactical. In our short attention span society, it stands as an extended, enthralling and thoughtful spectacle. Maybe I am just old fashioned? I can live with that.

I can't play cricket very well. I can't see the ball and I can't bowl. If I ever kept wicket, I might stop the occasional bye, but usually with a part of my body other than my gloved hands. But I love it! As a sport to watch and as I've got older, to listen to, on Test Match Special. It feels like everything is right with the world as you go about daily chores, with Jonathan Agnew or Michael Vaughan keeping you posted on the match.

Kennington Police had got themselves a control room inside the ground. It was located at the back of one of the stands with a fabulous view of the pitch. We were allowed to go there to have our snacks and to get a drink, but the boss on the day didn't want an entire serial of officers watching the game from this spectacular vantage point. I would have to find another spot.

On the Thursday, England batted first and to everyone's surprise, built up a sizeable score. By the time they were all out on the Friday, they had accumulated a total of 454. It must be stressed that despite my clear love of the game and wanting England to win, I was also very keen for the game to make it to the fifth day's play on Bank Holiday Monday. This would ensure not only did we avoid the Carnival, but we could sit back and watch the match on double time!

Surrey Cricket Club operate and run The Oval and at that time they were aware of the disturbance and delay caused by 'streakers' at the cricket. It was expected that at least one drunken punter would disrobe and then cavort across the pitch, tackle out. In years gone by there had been a number of these naked morons disrupting sporting events. For some reason at the cricket, it tended to be males and at the rugby, females. I've got no idea why that is! There had been famous pictures taken of a bloke hurdling the stumps at Lords and another of a chap after being caught, with his 'japscrackers' covered by a policeman's helmet. I didn't really fancy chasing one of these prats in full uniform to the languid amusement of the crowd, like some low point at The Roman Colosseum. To my relief, Surrey Cricket Club had brought in athletic sprinters from a local association and they were tasked with chasing and catching anyone foolish enough to try it. We were off the hook then!

The West Indies came out to bat on the Friday and went for it from the off. The weather was just about perfect and the two openers, Campbell and Benjamin began to score freely. They were scoring at a good rate too. Saturday could be a wonderful day's play. By now I had secured a seat right at the back of the stand opposite the main Pavilion. If I hunkered down in my seat with my helmet off, I was almost invisible. I did have a radio, so my skipper knew he could get hold of me, if I was needed. I might have spotted him watching from the other side of the bowler's arm. Anyway, next in to bat was a certain Brian Lara.

As I watched this legend of the game go about his business, a person in my row handed me a cushion to soften the hard, Oval seats. It became the most absorbing afternoon as the police radio stayed quiet and Brian Lara put on a show for that packed Saturday crowd. He eventually scored 179 off 206 deliveries, with 26 fours and just the one six. After he was out, the 'Windies' just kept on going, piling on the runs as Saturday turned into Sunday. Carl Hooper weighed in with a brilliant century of his own, supported by Captain Richie Richardson and Chanderpaul, batting as low as seven. As the Sunday wore on I was waiting, not for any disorder or streakers, but simply for the declaration to come.

692 for 8, the Windies finally declared late on that Sunday afternoon.

All England had to do to ensure my full days double time (sorry, to save the match) on the Monday, was to bat all day for the draw. My hopes weren't high. England's test match side could unravel really quickly and with Curtly Ambrose and Courtney Walsh steaming in, you would be forgiven for thinking it could all be over before lunch time. But thanks to the stoic determination of Michael Atherton, supported by Graham Thorpe and Graeme Hick, England managed to claw their way to the close of play on that fifth day and a wonderful draw. Honour was saved, the series was drawn, I had a lucrative Bank Holiday Monday in my pocket and had avoided Notting Hill for another year.

M. P. A. A.
(Metropolitan Police Athletic Association)

Does anyone play any sport? The Hendon instructor enquired.
"Hockey at school", I stated.
Details given, notes taken and information supplied.
Suddenly in week seven, my future in police sport was created.

A game at Crystal Palace; the summer league.
Representative sport; Wow! I was so proud.
My Hendon Classmates were full of intrigue.
An early finish to be able to play, is allowed.

Once on Borough, the system was explained.
You get four hour's time off to play each match.
If you were rest day, it was four hours gained.
But always exigencies of duty was the catch.

Men's hockey, the 4th team was where I played.
There were so many sports played by serving cops.
M.P.A.A sport. Get to play and be paid.
And the number abstracted did not hinder Ops.

It was the Duty Officer's call to allow time away.
With sufficient notice and numbers parading it wasn't refused.
Others on the Relief were also able to play.
A colleague competed in chess. MPAA time used.

Eventually I was promoted to the Men's 1st Eleven.
Sports colours awarded and several trophies won.
An incalculable number of positive impressions given.
What of MPAA sport now? It's virtually gone!

I first picked up a hockey stick at school, when I was eleven. I developed a reasonable talent for the sport and continued to play after finishing school. A season for Bournemouth and West Hampshire club, then all too soon I was off to Hendon to commence my police career. During one of the lessons in week seven, the instructor asked if any of us played any sport. One of my classmates spoke about his football and I put my hand up and mentioned hockey. The M.P.A.A (The Metropolitan Police Athletic Association) were looking for fresh sporting people in my intake. My details were passed on to the hockey section and after a few weeks I received an invitation.

The hockey team were playing an evening friendly the following week at Crystal Palace and I had been included in the team. It would require me leaving the class early to be able to get South of the river for the 6pm start. My instructor generously allowed me to leave the day's course early and off I went to play, travelling on a combination of Northern Line tube and buses to the sports ground.

At that time The Job gave every indication that they were keen for officers to be involved in representative sport and the M.P.A.A had a busy time with all the sports that officers were involved in. The Hockey section put out four Men's teams, all playing in the various leagues in Surrey as we played our home games at Imber Court Sports Club in Molesey. We played on grass pitches that had been marked out in the winter on the cricket out field.

Time off to play could be obtained if you were M.P.A.A. If you were playing on a day off you could add four hours on to your M.P.A.A card with the Duties Office. The same if you were playing after an Early shift or prior to reporting for Night Duty. If you were Late shift, you could have the first four hours off but would have to go into work after the game for 6-6.30pm. As I began to understand the system and started to accrue hours I would take all of the Saturday Late Turn off and, on most occasions, I would not go in for Night Duty.

Times were different, there were still so many officers parading that my abstraction to play sport was hardly noticed. There were one or two occasions when I had my time off request refused, but it was rare when I first started. It got progressively more difficult to get leave to play, as time went on.

To me, it was always a healthy thing to be doing. Playing sport with a different bunch of police mates, who came from all parts of London. We played in an open league against a variety of local club sides like, Goan, Sanderstead and Wallington. Most of the high street banks put out teams at that time too. Barclays had a really nice facility over near Ealing, Nat West had a sports ground near Streatham and the Bank of England had a fantastic set up in Roehampton Lane, the other side of Putney. I always thought we were showing the opposition teams that there was more to coppers than just upholding the law. We could show we were human by playing a game then socialising with them afterwards. I truly feel it was an incredibly positive way to promote police officers.

In addition to playing in our league there was the annual Police Athletic Association Cup tournament between different forces. A chance for the Met. team to test our mettle against other Constabularies in a knock-out trophy. When I started playing it was the Royal Ulster Constabulary (RUC) who were the pre-eminent hockey side. We ran them close a few times, but they always managed to come out on top. As time passed other sides came to the fore. Avon and Somerset had a useful outfit, Greater Manchester were always challenging for honours and The West Midlands were hard to beat. The added bonus of this competition was that the semi-finals and final would be hosted by a different Constabulary every year.

My first year to be selected to play, the Championship hosts were Lothian and Borders Police, up in Edinburgh. They put us up in a hotel overlooking the Forth road and rail bridges. We didn't win that year, but a splendid time was had by all and we had been given five days Special Leave, so it didn't eat into my annual leave allocation.

Another year the RUC hosted the tournament in Belfast. You had to hand it to those boys. They were able to play hockey to a really high standard, despite their professional Policing duties being by far, the most challenging in the UK. I had, and still have, the greatest of respect and admiration for those officers in Northern Ireland.

Eventually, as I was coming to the end of my involvement with Met. Police hockey we finally won the PAA cup when the tournament was hosted by Greater Manchester Police. After so many years of trying, it was a fitting time for me to move away from playing hockey for the police and try a fresh sporting challenge. This was not before being very proudly presented with Metropolitan Police Sports colours. I continued to play hockey until I had turned 50. I had moved to Sussex and after a hesitant start, I enjoyed many memorable years with Crowborough Hockey club, where I also met my wife, Paula.

We attended tournaments and festivals outside of the police too. The International Llanishen and Llandaff Hockey Festival, in Cardiff, Wales, was exceptional. My first experience of this wonderful long weekend of hockey was 1989. I remember it being that year because we were all in the bar of our hotel on the first night, just deciding where to go out for some food. On the television, Liverpool were about to be beaten by Arsenal in the dying seconds of the deciding game of that year's football league championship. You remember? That's the famous one that ended up being written about in the book 'Fever Pitch' by Nick Hornby.

That year I was still only 24 and playing on the right wing. I was never a naturally gifted hockey player but had learnt to hit the ball hard and could run fast with the ball under control. I never considered that I had high skill levels, but on one or two occasions throughout my career, I would do something that would surprise both me and the rest of the team. The Cardiff festival was one such moment. We were playing against a Warwickshire County invitational side, on an uneven grass pitch. I picked up the ball on the right and dribbled past two defenders into the D. I continued to dribble past defenders across the front of goal and off to the left of it. Then at the last moment, before I ran off the pitch, I reverse hit the ball into the roof of the net. I had never done that before and certainly never since. It was one of those. "Blimey! How did I do that?" moments.

I got selected for more games the following season. The selectors clearly thinking I was going to replicate this skill level on a regular basis. Sadly, I seldom did, but it is nice to have the memory of it. Cardiff was an annual opportunity for the disparate collection of police officers who made up our team and who worked all over London to come together, let off a little steam, have a very sociable weekend and play a few games of hockey with like-minded people.

We would also have one off games against representatives from other services and organisations. One such game was against the Fleet Air Arm at Yeovilton in Wiltshire. A friendly fixture that involved us driving down in a suitable bus and playing a game, enjoying a sociable evening in Yeovil and then returning the following day. By now I was qualified to drive a police carrier and our fleet of unmarked minibuses. I was also the one tasked to arrange transport.

Having arranged the use of a vehicle to take our team down to Yeovil, I was told to collect it from the vehicle depot in Lambeth. The logbook and keys would be left at the second-floor reception for me. The Lambeth depot is a busy place and when I attended and got the lift to the second floor there was an office full of people working at their desks behind the lady at reception. I explained who I was and she began hunting for the logbook I was there to collect. After a little while she returned and asked who I had spoken to. Luckily, I had the name on a piece of paper and she once more went off to hunt for the logbook.

"You'll have to take this one, it's the only one available now, as some extra aid commitments have altered some vehicle allocations", the slightly flustered receptionist suggested.

"Ok, I understand, can I just take your name as authorising the change?" I asked. My thinking was if it all goes pear shaped I have this lady's name as giving me the vehicle.

"It's Mandy", she replied and handed me a black logbook, which I opened to reveal the ignition key inside. I put the key in my pocket and the logbook in my rucksack. Remember, she handed the logbook and ignition key to me.

I got the lift down to sub level two where the vehicles were parked neatly in lines. I pulled out the key and read the registration number off the fob. Now it was a case of hunting for the corresponding vehicle. No locking mechanism or alarm on the fob, so a walk around the car park until I found it.

Well, it was a marked carrier for starters, blue lights and a Met. sound siren inside. It was fairly beaten up, with several dents and scuffs around the body work, but most of the carriers were like this. The tyres looked sound and inflated. I got in and started the engine first time, sounded a bit rough, so I got the logbook out to check the last time it was used. Ok, not been used for a month, just let it warm up a bit. Mileage was accurate with the figure signed for by the previous driver. The damage section was pretty much out of room, but as I read through the litany of dents, scratches and dinks, there didn't seem to be anything too serious. The engine was now sounding normal and there were no warning lights on the dash, so off I went.

I had arranged to pick up the team from Imber Court Sports Club. I cruised down the A3 and off into East Molesey, parked up and wandered into the bar to find them. I wasn't late, so they were still on their first pint.

"Let's go!" I greeted the boys.

"What the fucking hell is this?" one of the chaps said pointing to the marked police Mercedes Sprinter carrier.

"It's what they gave me, Lambeth said they had extra aid or something", I said laughing.

Off we went, keeping to the speed limit and NOT using the blue lights or two tones....honestly!

We arrived in good time for the fixture and having been allocated a small barrack room, changed into our kit and went off to play. It was a great game, played in the best of spirits. We thought we had them, but in the end, a draw seemed a fair result and we had been invited to join the opposition for dinner in Yeovil. The dinner was fine but the nightclub afterwards was probably a mistake. We did get back to our barracks in time for several hours sleep.

In the morning, one of my teammates who was also qualified to drive the carrier suggested that it might be preferable for him to drive us back up to London. We all piled in and he got behind the wheel and did his pre-flight checks. Opening the logbook, he pulled the buff-coloured book out of the black leather wallet, revealing it's cover for the first time. He turned and handed the book to me. There in bold red letters on a piece of paper glued to the cover were the words.

DO NOT DRIVE ON A PUBLIC ROAD

"Ah! Well, err! We're here now and I got us down here, you'll be ok to get us back?"

I am not sure I heard his reply over the engine starting and the laughter from the rest of the team. We got back to London without incident and I took over the driving to return the carrier to Lambeth. I parked it where I had found it in sub-basement two and got the lift back up to the reception. Mandy looked up from her desk.

I placed the logbook on her desk, having reversed the buff interior book, so the cover wasn't visible. She smiled as I thanked her and I bid her farewell and got to the lifts. As I waited Mandy arrived.

"You took the wrong vehicle", she looked a little concerned.

"Actually, you handed me the wrong vehicle log book," I countered, as the lift doors opened.

I got into the lift, turned and looked at her. I smiled as the doors started to close and I like to think she smiled back as she disappeared from view. I never heard about it or got any grief over it, which always surprised me.

In addition to MPAA sport there was some healthy sporting contests contested at Divisional level. Battersea had a very strong and keen football section. One of the CID officers set up the Battersea Divisional Rugby Society (WARS) and some truly memorable fixtures were played. One particularly memorable trip to The Mumbles in Swansea really deserves a chapter alone, but I feel I am straying off topic.

Another subject probably in need of a book of its own would have to be the Battersea Divisional Cricket side's annual 'Wessex Tour'.

Centering in Lyme Regis, Dorset and playing several fixtures in the area against Axminster, Uplyme and All Saint's clubs. A quite remarkable and wonderful excursion that will require a multitude of permissions for any further mention.

Sport played a very important role within the police. I would like to think it continues to do so to this day. It offered something else. At a time when the police are so scrutinized it might be useful to get some media coverage of officers engaging in sporting pursuits?

Take His Arm!

A man has severed his arm in a fall.
We blast to the address in Altenburg Gardens.
The male has put his arm through a window in the hall.
The wife is screaming. Shoved aside, no pardons.

Tourniquet applied, elevate the arm, an ambulance has been called.
The air is thick with the coppery smell of claret.
The ambulance is taking too long his treatment is stalled.
Ignoring protocol, it's into Whisky One, our blue lighted chariot.

We message ahead that we are on route to St. Tommy's.
Lying across the back seat the victim is just about conscious.
The Duty Officer is informed. His mood is stormy.
Such a mundane accident. Reminds us life is precious.

We fly up to the A & E main entrance.
A team of experts relieve us of our victim.
We assess the time taken. He has a chance.
Doctors, consultants and surgeons worked to save his limb.

The Duty Officer begins his rebuke in the hospital car park.
Our shirt sleeve order looks a bloodied mess.
If we delayed, he would be dead. Fuck that for a lark.
Still stuck on for disobeying an order, no less!

Sometimes in life, instinct takes over and you just act without thinking. I was by now relishing my time as a Class One Driver (didn't I mention it? Class One mate!). Enjoying yet another posting driving Whisky One. I used to enjoy a punt onto surrounding Divisions, just stretching my legs, so to speak, while learning the streets of a larger area of London than just Battersea. A little foray down to Tooting and Clapham's areas. A cheeky drift across the river to Chelsea for a mooch down the Kings and Fulham Roads.

On one particular Late Turn I was just returning from a Chelsea excursion heading South over Battersea Bridge, just about to turn into the Nick for a brew.

"Whisky One and all units, a male with serious injuries from a fall in Altenburg Gardens"!

"Whisky One!", my operator took the call immediately. Yeah, we'll have some of that!

"Ambulance has been called, Whisky Alpha, over.

"Received, Whisky One".

Altenburg Gardens was a residential street that ran North to South between Lavender Hill and the South Circular. Lots of large Victorian terraced houses and owner occupiers. Not somewhere we would normally be called to. On came the lights and noise and off we went. Hammered past the Nick down Battersea Bridge Road, screaming left into Prince of Wales Drive, then an acute right turn in Cambridge Road to get me down to the lights at Battersea Park Road. This is the junction where I smashed the van into that 2CV and ended up gripping the rail, so a degree of caution used, then across and away South down Latchmere Road.

In the 1970's cop show 'The Sweeney' they were always using Latchmere Road for their car chases. A particular part of this street is the tight chicane in the road as it goes under the railway, just past Sheepcote Lane. This always looked spectacular in the cop show. In reality it was tight, with no visibility and had to be taken with care. Not today! Got past a van coming the other way by at least a fag paper and on up to Lavender Hill. A right then second left into Altenburg Gardens. My operator is out with the first aid kit as I pull up. I flipped the car round facing the way we had come and scrambled out of the car and ran up to the open door.

My colleague was now bent over a figure lying prone at the top of the stairs. It was actually a landing at a bend in their stairs. A lady was stood higher up on the stairs frantic and sobbing. I got up there and passed my partner, who by now had fitted a tourniquet high on the victim's right arm. There was a lot of blood. Like someone had opened a tin of red paint and thrown it up in the air. I got to the lady and she just pointed to the smashed French door that led from their stair landing on to a small balcony. Fairly easy to work out. Her husband had been rushing down the stairs, lost his footing and stumbled. He put his right arm out to break his fall and put it straight through the glass French windows on the bend in their stairs. Ouch!

There was blood everywhere and my operator's white shirt looked like he'd done a shift at an abattoir.

"Whisky One on scene. Male has a serious injury, how long for the ambulance, over."

"Whisky One, stand by", the Nick began trying to find the answer for me.

The wife was now slumped on the stairs, head in her hands as we tried to slow the bleed with the tourniquet and elevating the arm. The bloke was still conscious but very pale.

"Whisky Alpha, anything? Whisky One over".

"Stand by".

That's when you have to decide. I knew the protocol. *He should go in an ambulance. We should try and stabilise him as best we can until the ambulance crew arrive.* But I've got a wife on the stairs watching us fumble about trying to stop blood pissing everywhere. The bloke is going to lose consciousness soon. I am not getting any information about the ETA of the ambulance. This is all my call.

"Whisky Alpha, we're going to take him to Tommy's in the car, over".

"Negative, Whisky One. Wait for the ambulance".

Quite rightly, the senior Controller, a Sergeant, had gone with protocol and ordered me to stay at the address and wait for the ambulance. It's one of those moments where you have to make the call yourself. I am the one on scene. I have to decide. Wait for the ambulance, which may be too late for our victim, or throw him in the back of the Area Car and get him to the hospital ourselves. Watch him die on the stairs (possibly) or break the rules, disobey an order and risk taking him in the back of our car.

"We going to take him now, Whisky One, over" and we somehow got him down the stairs and outside.

"Whisky one, received", no more arguing at least.

I told the wife we were going to St. Thomas' Hospital in Westminster.

My operator got in the back with the bloke, who we now knew as Alan. He was laid across my colleague's lap, who was able to keep the right arm raised a little.

I got in behind the wheel.

"Hold tight". Off we went.

When you drive at speed with the noise and lights going, you give it the beans, obviously. But sometimes you give it maybe seven or eight tenths, holding a little something back and assess the risks in your driving plan. At this stage of my police career, I was young, keen and with a fairly naive view of the police and doing the job to the best of my ability. When I turned right out of Altenburg Gardens into Lavender Hill and flicked all the switches I was determined to give it everything. Ten tenths as I roared past Lavender Hill Nick and down towards the Wandsworth Road.

There are so many junctions and hazards in the Wandsworth Road. Parked and moving traffic, pedestrians ambling across the road. Loss of vision under bridges as I kept the car offside in the oncoming lane, forcing that traffic out of my way. Getting past another bus and back on to my side of the road as we neared Vauxhall Cross. Through a red light there, serious swerve and drift it back to avoid a motorist who hasn't seen me.

"Alright in the back, sorry".

"Keep going, Guy!" my operator screams.

Past Vauxhall Bridge, then the MI6 building as we hurtle along the embankment. I remember the double flash of a speed camera just past Tintagel House and then we slewed round Lambeth Bridge roundabout. Less traffic as we flew along Lambeth Palace Road and finally up the ramp to the Accident and Emergency department at St. Thomas Hospital. I wasn't necessarily on the clock, but I reckon I'd got there in about five minutes. It was a four-mile run that would normally take about twenty to twenty-five minutes at that time of day.

The A & E at the hospital knew we were coming and were waiting for us as we slammed to a stop. A team of scrubs-clad staff got Alan out of the back of the car and put him on a trolley and quickly wheeled him away inside.

My operator came over and smiled at me. He was literally covered in blood.

"Did we hit anything on our way?" I asked him.

"I don't think so".

I looked at him, a bit like Paddington Bear and smiled.

"No, we didn't hit anything".

"What about vicinity only's".

"Nope, none".

"Good answer, thanks".

He praised me on the drive and we went inside to check on our patient.

Initially we had to reassure the nurses and other staff that neither of us were injured and that it was our patient's blood all over us. Alan had been taken straight into surgery, so there was nothing more we could do. One of my colleagues on the Relief had gone to Altenburg Gardens after we had left and scooped up the wife and he walked into the foyer of A & E with her as we were leaving. She looked over at us and nodded, then hurried away to be with her husband.

I got fairly used to getting torn off a strip in The Job. I will concede that I was quite often obstinate and difficult to manage. If I was being tasked by a certain type of senior officer our styles would sometimes clash. Clearly this particular day's work was a case in point.

We had a protocol that we should follow when it came to transporting seriously injured victims to hospital. Simply put, they should always go in an ambulance. Both the Controller at Battersea and my Duty Officer had quite rightly ordered me to wait for the ambulance, rather than take the victim in the back of the Area Car. But on this occasion, I genuinely felt that the risk of waiting for transport was outweighed by the risk to life of the man with his arm hanging off. I will never know what might have happened if I had waited. He may well have survived and got better treatment on the way to hospital, but it was an 'on the scene' instant judgement call.

My Duty Officer was livid and when my colleague and I walked back out of the A & E, heading to our vehicle, he was waiting. His stance and the colour of his face was a giveaway. Oh! and the steam escaping from his ears. To his credit he had a conversational style of delivering a bollocking. He never raised his voice, but simply spoke his piece about following orders, disciplined service, maverick RT drivers etc. I sometimes knew when to shut up and I just listened to his speech. My only reply was to suggest I had acted in what I thought were the victim's best interests and I appreciated the risks and the protocols when I made my decision.

I stuck to this when I was sitting across the desk from the Superintendent, with my Duty Officer and the Controller sat next to me, in the informal setting of the Superintendent's office. The 'Super' was a lovely chap, with a wealth of practical experience and he listened to all sides of the story.

As I'm writing this I can't help but remember that line between Ronnie Corbett and Ronnie Barker, when they are both dressed in police uniform.

"Morning Super!"

"Hello Wonderful!".

Always makes me chuckle. Anyway…

Luckily, I felt he was keen to keep the situation in house and not involve the chaps from Five Area complaints. We discussed my behaviour, not just this incident but several other occasions when I had perhaps overstepped my authority. Reading the room, I duly ate a large slice of humble pie and promised to do better in future. I don't think either of my Duty Officer and the Controller wanted to escalate the matter either and I was given a final warning (again) not to ignore and or disobey lawful orders from senior officers.

The Jumper

Always on a Sunday! A woman has fallen from a tower block.
Despatched to the scene. Operator searches for a body.
Up to the 10th floor. Two distraught males in shock.
My colleague calls for the Duty Officer. A body in the lobby.

Inside the flat with the ex-boyfriend and victim's father.
The victim had attended, unable to handle the boyfriend's rejection.
Hours of pleading and talking end with some laughter.
Both men feel her mood is heading in the right direction.

Tea is being made. She excuses herself to use the toilet.
Boyfriend realises the truth too late and heads up the stairs.
He sees her sitting on the ledge, her mind is set.
He rushes forward as she jumps! Utter despair.

The body crashes through a glass lobby roof.
Severing the victim's legs and her head.
Photographic attend. The CID are satisfied with the truth.
The victim moved. Where's the head? A frantic search is led.

Full statements taken. First on scene goes with the body to the mortuary.
Not before the missing head is found under a nearby car.
The Council wash away the blood. The family await an enquiry.
Reflection over a pint. Do these calls leave a scar?

Let me say at the outset of this particular job. It wasn't one of mine. By the time this horrific incident happened I had moved to the Training Unit. One of my roles was to plan, devise and present classes to the working Beat Duty officers on the Division. I decided to prepare some work on scene preservation and went hunting for some suitable examples. One such set of photographs and attached report that came across my desk was the one which I write about now. As it's a third-party story, I apologise for any details I may miss, but I gleaned sufficient from the report to write it down here.

The Winstanley estate was a frequent venue for police to attend. A large sprawling estate of tower and other low-level blocks of flats. At the time of this incident some of the former council blocks had been bought up, given a lick of paint and some new windows. A brick wall and entry phone gates were put around them so they could be sold off as luxury apartments, walking distance from Clapham Junction Station.

The events that led to the call had started in the middle of the Saturday night, the week before. A male living in one block, on the 10th floor of the fifteen-storey building had been seeing a girl for several months and as he made clear in his subsequent statement she had become both ultra-possessive and paranoid. They were both young professional people in their twenties and it was getting to be more of an intense relationship than he wanted. She lived over in Clapham with her parents and would spend many evenings with him at the flat.

As time went on, the man felt he was now in a relationship that was beyond what he wanted and knew that trying to extricate himself from the situation was going to be tricky. He was lucky enough to have met his girlfriend's father and they had got on reasonably well. Enough to suggest to him that he felt the time had come to end the relationship with the daughter.

When he told the girl, it did not go well. He was able to take her home to her father in his car. She was distraught, in tears of despair, then violent anger, but somehow, he was able to get her inside the house in Clapham and drove away hoping the girl would quickly recover from the rejection. But he had seriously misjudged the mental state of his former girlfriend.

The phone calls started that same evening, ringing in the middle of the night. The calls began with pleading, then became abusive as he refused to change his mind. Then he began getting similar calls at work, until he had to get the company operator to block them coming through. He called the father, who was also aware of how his daughter had become so obsessive with the man. The father said he was trying to arrange counselling for his daughter, he was so concerned. After the rest of the working week finished the man had spent a quiet Saturday at home doing chores.

At about 8pm on that Saturday evening the entry phone buzzer sounded. It was the girl, in an obviously very distressed state, screaming and crying into the entry phone. He felt he had no option than to buzz her in and try and placate her in person. He did mention in his statement that in hindsight he wondered if he should have gone down to her and talk to her outside. But like most of us he thought it better to keep matters private, rather than play out some vitriolic argument in the street.

She came upstairs and there began the hours of tortuous arguing and tears, coupled with rage and silence. All the time the man felt he was getting nowhere and the girl was getting more and more unhinged. By now it was almost midnight and there seemed no end or resolution in sight. The man was by now also worried about the mental state of the girl and excused himself to ring her father.

About forty-five minutes later, according to statements, the father attended and the two males now tried to calm the woman down. There were moments when they thought they were succeeding, only for the female to suddenly swing from anguished sobbing to stubborn anger. The hours wore on as the men tried to be rational. Both say in their statements that they should have called someone by now, as their efforts seemed to clearly have been in vain. During a brief lull in the pleading and bargaining they made a catastrophic mistake and left the girl alone. While dad was phoning his wife, the former boyfriend was making yet another cup of tea.

By now it was almost 5.30am in the morning, a long night of very emotionally draining discussion and placation. When the man returned with the tea, she was gone, the front door left wide open. The man states that he knew instantly what this meant and had a sixth sense of where he thought the girl had gone. He could see the floor numbers above the lift door rising as he raced towards the stairs. The block had 15th floors and he raced up the five flights of stairs as fast as he was able.

As he came to the last flight he remembers he took a breath, before once more racing to the top and reaching the landing of the 15th Floor. He could see the girl now sat on the sill of the landing window. A great big window, that could inexplicably be opened fully. She was sat with her feet up on the ledge and the large window, wide open. Chillingly in his statement he describes how he was frozen to the spot, breathing heavily from the exertion of climbing five flights of stairs. He clearly saw the girl staring back at him. He had no opportunity for any further discussion. As he looked at her, she fixed him with a cold stare and without a single word simply leaned away from him and fell out of the window. Gone.

He stood there, rooted to the spot for several minutes before slowly making his way back downstairs to his flat, where he firstly had to break the news to her father. Before real shock took over he was able to make the call to the police and wait quietly for them to arrive.

It was the Sunday Early Turn, Whisky One picked up the call and made their way swiftly to the scene. A quick cursory search around the outside of the block did not make it immediately obvious where a body was. Both officers attended the flat and after hearing the story from the man and the girl's father they went up to the 15th floor landing and took a look out of the window. Looking down they immediately saw the almost body shaped hole in the perspex and iron domed canopy of the fire exit stair well.

The Duty Officer and the CID had been informed and attended to both interview and take statements from the two men in the flat. The crew of Whisky One were the first officers to go to the stairwell. The girl's body had crashed through the perspex roof and the red iron framework had severed both of her legs below the knee. She landed on the stairs face down with her arms raised above her shoulders obscuring the head. The officers both mention the incongruity of seeing the girl's feet still wearing Kicker boots, positioned on the stairs some distance from the rest of the body. A pretty horrific scene.

There was some waiting time to get a Scene of Crime Officer (SOCO) on a Sunday morning, but eventually one attended. One of the virtues of it being so early on a Sunday was it minimised the number of 'Disaster Groupies' who turned out. Plus, the block was private, so they couldn't get inside the gates anyway. The ambulance crew had attended and did the decent thing and said they would wait and convey the body to hospital when SOCO had finished.

Eventually the decision was made to move the body and the two paramedics moved forward and rolled the girl on to her front.

"Err! Officer, where's the head?

"What"?

As the medics had rolled the body over and lowered the arms it was clear that the head had been severed in the fall, but it was not inside the stairwell with the rest of the body. Other units were now also on scene and they all began a thorough, if rather morbid, hunt for the victim's head. After a short while, one of the officers saw a fleck of blood on the bonnet of a car parked close to the stairwell. Closer examination saw that the bonnet was also dented. He followed the natural curve of the bonnet down to the front of the car and the wall it was parked in front of. Leaning over the low wall he saw the severed head of the young girl resting against the brickwork.

One of the Scenes of Crime specialists worked out that it was to do with physics. As the body crashed through the roof, the torso and legs had sufficient weight and velocity to go through into the stairwell. The head was severed, but somehow didn't go through and at the point of it severing, had actually bounced free of the rest of the body, rolled off the domed roof of the stairwell, bounced off the bonnet of the car, rolled off the front of it and over the low wall coming to rest where it did.

I used the incident to help officers understand that sometimes a scene of crime can be a changing and evolving thing as the investigation gets underway. The sadness of the story also provided a useful commentary to my colleagues that there is always a very human side to what we deal with.

Back in the canteen, the crew of Whisky One were writing some notes and mulling over what they had just dealt with. The eventual discovery of the head had been an interesting development. A colleague sat having a brew wondered what might have happened if the head hadn't been found so expediently. Knowing the Winstanley Estate well, I did wonder if one of the many stray dogs could have happened upon it by chance and the next thing we hear are reports of a dog running through the estate with a human head in its mouth? That leads very nicely to another horrific Winstanley Estate crime scene.

Murder and Suicide

A woman has been forced on to the game.
The pimp comes around to make his threat.
She had paid her dues, but still he came.
Now her blood has been shed and the walls are wet.

He fired the sawn off in a sudden rage!
She was stood in the hallway as he blasted.
Point blank range with his manly twelve gauge.
Dead where she fell, his meal ticket ended.

He takes the gun and maybe felt remorse.
So, into the lounge then he shoots himself as well.
His aim is poor. Somehow, he survives, of course.
Just his face on the ceiling, the rest is going to hell.

First officers on scene survey the savage blood and gore.
Gun moved to the television; the ambulance takes the male away.
They preserve the scene; these uniforms know the score.
It's time for an AFO, CID and Duty Officer to have their say.

The male at hospital lived for a further thirteen hours.
A face blown off is hard to survive.
Two bodies now lie on the mortuary slab. No flowers.
Policing the Winstanley. It's good to be alive!

Another routine patrol on the Winstanley Estate in Battersea. Two officers were called to a flat in one of the blocks on the Estate. Sounds of gunshots. This vast, eight storey block, a rabbit warren of broken lifts and clammy stairwells was visited frequently, like most of the blocks on the Winstanley. The officers carefully entered through an unlatched front door, having spotted the prone feet and lower legs of a person. As they got to the business end of the entrance hall, they saw the first victim.

A mixed-race female in her late twenties to early thirties was lying half in the hall, and half in the kitchen, with her torso and head wedged against the kitchen door. She had a huge hole in the side of her head, the contents of which was dribbling down the white gloss paint of the door. Not being experts, the two officers were still able to see that this injury was the result of a gun shot at point blank range, to the side of the head. Again, not being experts, they could not officially state that she was dead, but safe to say there were no life signs. The head had been distorted by the blast and there was blue wadding from the projectile embedded in the wound.

I am amazed at the bravery and stoicism of the two Beat Duty officers, who, despite clear evidence of the use of firearms, continued their search of the premises. They stepped past the bloodied corpse of the female and slowly entered the lounge. Face down on the floor was a black male of indeterminate age, motionless, with blood coming from a head wound. One officer immediately felt for a pulse and found a faint rhythm. The two turned the male on to his back, this released from his grasp the sawn-off double-barrelled shot gun he had been holding. One officer wearing gloves gingerly picked up the weapon and placed it conspicuously on top of the television, to await it being made safe by an authorised firearms officer (AFO).

It's perhaps time to mention that at one stage of my service, I carried a firearm on the streets of London. I did my three-week firearms course at Lippitts Hill in Essex. Trained to use, maintain and fire a Glock 17 pistol. It was a necessary part of my role as a newly appointed Royalty and Diplomatic Protection Officer. But perhaps more of those stories another time. The firearms course was, as it should be, a serious affair. It is incredibly important to soak up as much information and to pass the firearms course as well as you can. In the first instance you have to be a good shot, to be able to hit sections of the target almost all the time to pass.

I remember incurring the wrath of my instructor on the day we spent having a look at the miscellaneous weapons they have at the training centre. First the pump action shot gun. I wanted to rack it one handed, like in the movies, that didn't go down well. Then the Walther PPK, everyone doing their dreadful impersonations of James Bond (the Sean Connery one, obviously). Then the Luger pistol, generated a round of Gestapo impressions. "We haf vays of making you talk" etc. Finally, they had a Winchester repeating rifle, with the lever action. Now as a film fan, one of my all-time favourites is True Grit (the John Wayne one of 1969). He somehow spins the rifle after each firing with one hand activating the lever mechanism so he can fire again. When I embarked on trying this in the confines of the classroom environment, I was very nearly struck from the course.

You also have to make the right judgement and the course tries hard to simulate ways in which they can make you decide what to do under stressful conditions.

The firearms people had several different ways to try to teach and manage judgement. At my time, one such tool was an indoor range with a sort of tracing paper target. It formed a white screen where prepared videos could be projected. The idea was that each of the candidates on the course would be armed with a blue Glock 17 that had been converted to fire small paint pellets. So effectively indoor paintballing. The video scenario would play out in front of the candidate under instruction and he or she would have to decide when, and if, they might have to use their firearm.

It's a training course and as a candidate you expect to have to fire at some stage. My turn. I am faced with a male shouting the odds at me, almost screaming. I can't see one of his hands, which is slightly behind his back. I should say, you are allowed to verbalise and challenge the action, as you would in reality. I shouted, declaring I was an armed police officer and that he should show me his hands. I now have my firearm drawn and am aiming at the male. His arm comes suddenly into view and he has his fingers arranged in that faux position of index finger pointed at me, thumb up. Fuck me! I could easily have shot him for being armed with his fingers

The scenario carries on and walking towards him is a female pushing a pram. Of course, there is, it's a training scenario like out of Men in Black, or similar. The male won't keep his hands visible, despite my shouts for him to do so. Now he's arguing with the female and somehow his body is obscured by the pram. Before I have time to make another challenge, he points a gun at me and fires a split second before I do. Fucking Hell! The scene has frozen and the tracing paper screen has taken my paint pellet and I have shot the male in the chest. Phew!

Some other candidates did their scenes, different to mine, but we all seemed to do ok at the de-brief.

It was then that we heard the story of one of the candidates, who shall we say at no point went on to carry a firearm as a police officer.

Like all of us at the tracing paper screen target, he was watching his scenario play out. According to the way the story was told, he was incredibly nervous and had been struggling with much of the course anyway. I don't recall which scene was playing on his video target, but so the legend has it, he pretty much blasted away at everything and anything moving. He shot two male passers-by, the postman, a pregnant mother and her toddler, the armed male and a dog!

As the dust settled and he realised that he's failed that test, most likely the entire course and might be lucky to even remain a police officer, he gets a moment of clarity and turns to the two instructors sat open mouthed in their chairs and without pause, aims and fires a paint round at each, hitting them both in the centre of their chests.

"What the fucking hell do you think you are doing Officer?"

"Well……. I didn't want any witnesses!"

He then slowly placed the Glock on a desk and left the range, Lippitts Hill and possibly the UK.

Enough of this levity, back to matey, face down, without a face, on the lounge floor of a flat on the Winstanley Estate.

The male had an horrific wound. His nose and one eye were missing. One of the officers saw lots of shotgun pellets embedded in the ceiling above the male, along with bits of his nose and other facial debris. It looked to the untrained eye like the male had held the gun under his chin and at the point of firing, the majority of the shot missed him, but enough to blast the front of his face off, rather than his entire head. An ambulance was called.

By the time the suits from CID appeared, the male had been conveyed by ambulance to hospital. An AFO attended to make the sawn off on the television safe.

Talking of shotguns (the double-barrelled variety), reminds me of a job we overheard on the mains set radio in Whisky One. We had got ourselves assigned to a job taking place on Fulham's ground, on one of their estates. Loads of units were going to the call. I don't think we were too far away when we heard the following over the radio.

"MP, MP. Yeah, we've got nostrils on the plot down 'ere, can we have a gunship, over?"

Accuracy, brevity and speed…remember?

There was a slight pause before another unit chimed in.

"Can we have a CID translator too? I believe firearms have been seen and my esteemed CID colleague is requesting an Armed Response vehicle to the scene, over".

I'd never heard such a concise description of a double-barrelled shotgun before. Nostrils! Brilliant. Always brings a smile.

Back at the murder scene, the CID, Duty Officer, Scenes of Crime Officer, photographer and Uncle Tom Cobley were all now in attendance. They were trying to piece together what had happened in this flat, in the middle of a residential block. Units at the hospital remained with the male, who never regained consciousness and died about thirteen hours after the shooting.

The eventual story was quite simple. The female who lived at the flat was an escort who worked a selection of West End hotels. She considered herself to be independent and not beholden to anyone. However, she had a former boyfriend, more like her pimp really, who found out she was still escorting but not passing the proceeds on to him, as she had done previously.

He had attended the flat in an attempt to persuade her that he ought to be receiving his cut of her takings. It is suggested that the discussion became heated and, in an effort to make his point more forcefully, he pulled out the sawn-off shotgun he had brought with him. Whether he meant to shoot the female or just threaten her, will never be known. If she was his potential meal ticket it would perhaps seem foolish to cut off that income supply, but in the heat of the moment? You just don't know!

The shotgun was fired with the gun barrels touching the side of her head. After that it can only be surmised what went through the male's head, that is, before shotgun pellets. Maybe he felt remorse and anguish for what he had done and decided to take his own life? Did he panic and decide he couldn't face the prospect of a lengthy jail sentence? Again, it will never be known.

What was established, was that at the point of firing he pulled away ever so slightly, so that a portion of the shell's pellets missed him entirely and embedded themselves in the ceiling. If he'd fired true he would have blown his entire head off, instead the projectiles in the cartridge carved away the front of his face.

That call was taken as another routine Beat Duty job. Another in the huge variety of stuff the uniform Beat Duty officers deal with. Of course, they then call everyone else to take it over, task and investigate, but they go in first.

That's all about being a Beat Duty Officer. You take one call, then the next. After finishing their notes about the murder and suicide on the Winstanley, they might have gone to report a burglary and sat with victims of that particular crime. They might have been trying to sort out youths being twats or just in at the Nick having some refreshments. It was an extreme call to take, but it was just the next job on the CAD (computer aided despatch) to be dealt with.

Officer Safety

It used to be six laps of the Hendon track.
Now it's a fifteen-metre sprint against the bleep.
A fitness test to stop us being slack.
Just get to level five, then you can sleep.

Officer Safety training for all, to rank of Chief Inspector.
Working in pairs, so that you look out for each other
A module developing contact and cover.
In reality, there were always insufficient available to bother.

Rigid handcuff training. There were too many moves!
Keeping it simple the varieties reduced to four.
Suspects are either High Risk or Unknown Risk, which proves,
In my opinion; Cuff everyone to even the score.

Palm heel strikes. Use of elbow and knee.
Sweeping kicks and toe punts to the shin.
Take on the padded suited man with glee.
Keep going to the end, he might let you win.

Finally beat the living daylights out of a mannequin.
Use of batons on muscle groups and joints.
Once more into the ring with the padded man.
Upper, lower and backhand strikes will all gain you points.

Way back at Training School, in the spring of 1986 I once ran six laps around the 400 metres track in 7 minutes and 55 seconds. Not world beating, but certainly well within the twelve and a bit minutes we were expected to do it in, to pass the fitness test. That was pretty much it as regards a fitness test in those days. Fast forward to the back end of my service and there was the sudden implementation of a force fitness test. Quite right too, but many years too late in my opinion. It is absolutely imperative that police officers should be fit and healthy, as they go about their duties.

One of the new requirements was a bleep test. For the uninitiated, it is a 15-metre distance that you walk, then trot, then run, then sprint between until you can go no further. You time your speed, so that you arrive at the end of the 15 metres on the sound of a bleep, that gets progressively quicker, as the levels increase. There were different levels for different departments. The TSG and firearms had to reach a higher level than Beat Duty Officers. I can't remember what the level for Beat Duty was, quite low though. I think they had to make it low for fear of too many 'lardy' officers failing it. Also built into the day was defensive officer safety stuff, involving use of handcuffs and ASP's (gravity friction lock batons…. the ones that extend when you whip them out!).

You were supposed to do a day of this every six months or it may have been once a year, it was hard to know. This was largely because my admin unit kept failing to update my file and I used to get a squib every so often, telling me my Officer Safety Training was out of date. After initially telling them I'd only been the previous week, I eventually got bored with their poor filing and just went every time they suggested and had a day of Officer Safety again. Towards the end of my service, I actually got quite fit and reasonably good at handcuffing people, because I seemed to be there most months.

At training school, we did a little bit of basic Aikido defensive stuff. I've never been a Ninja. I am not really co-ordinated enough to be able to tie someone in knots with the Bruce Lee stuff. I always found that when I was rolling around on the floor with a prisoner it was hard to be able to remember, let alone implement some fantastical martial art move. They also did a session of 'milling' with us in the boxing gym. I mentioned it earlier, but it involved the instructors putting two of us, of equal size and weight in the ring and letting us go at it. I do recall they took the female officers out of the class for that bit. I don't know why? As if a scrote gives a toss about whether the officer he or she hits, is female or not!

It got me to experience what getting hit in the face feels like, or in my case, repeatedly hit in the face. My opponent had 'done a bit', as he told me afterwards as I staunched my bloody nose. The bottom line, is that getting hit in the face hurts. It disorients you and can seriously impair judgement and the ability to defend yourself. My abiding memory of milling was sufficient to try and avoid being hit in the face for the next thirty years, if possible.

Out on the streets, the other thing that surprised me was that when the general public cut up rough and need to be detained in some way, they never behaved in the way my 'opponent' in the training environment did. Trying to caution someone you have arrested as they literally throw you about like a rag doll. Trying to handcuff a prisoner who has massive arms and such strength, that as I get one bracelet on his muscular wrist, he lifts me fully off the ground. The public can be awkward, strong, wilful, bat-shit-crazy and ultimately very difficult to subdue in a Home Office approved manner. You did what you could to not only detain the person, but to do it with minimal injury to both you and your colleagues. It did mean that I learned to not fight fair. To sometimes wait for overwhelming numbers of my colleagues to turn up, get in the first blow, or to go to a call mob handed in the first place.

I went to a domestic in a flat. Another one! The female victim was ok, no stabs wounds, just a swollen face from the most recent flurry of punches her husband had inflicted upon her. I could hear the chap crashing about in the kitchen. As I entered the small space it was immediately clear he'd had a drink. I knew he needed nicking; the question was how do I, all 5' 10" and about 12 stone (back then, dear readers) get to grips with this six foot plus drunken yob?

Shock and awe! I don't know why, but I decided to charge him, a sort of pre-emptive strike with my whole body. It took him by surprise and as he was bent back over the table I made a grab for him. So now we are wrestling in the kitchen and not good wrestling either. He's sort of got me around the waist and as I freed my arms I was able to get him in a really good headlock in the crook of my left arm and holding that arm with my right hand, I wondered what to do next. I had colleagues with me, but there was no space in the kitchen to get anyone else in there at that moment. I spotted a massive stockpot on the stove and in an instant, I ran at the stove, ramming his head into the saucepan, which gave a satisfying 'clang' as we bounced back together from it. This brought him to the ground, allowing two colleagues to join the fray and successfully cuff him. Textbook!

I went to an address on the Doddington Estate with my colleague who had the maniacal laugh. He would have been driving, because he had more service than me, which he always did! We get to a flat and a female has gone berserk and attacked her husband. Honestly! She carried on attacking him, even when we were inside the address trying to talk to them both. She was about five foot four, skinny and bonkers. I made a grab for her as she was kicking out at her partner. Somehow, she wriggled out of my grip, at the same time wriggling out of her top and her bra. Don't ask me how, but I am now trying to subdue a topless female, going (more) berserk!

All I can hear is the fucking laugh from my colleague, which intensifies as the family pet, a large German Shepherd, makes its presence known by biting me on the backside. He briefly stops laughing to make good her arrest and we leave the scene. He steals my arrest while I am detained at St. Thomas' Hospital getting a tetanus injection, which hurt more than the bloody dog bite!

Can you see a pattern? It's not easy to react to things in an approved Home Office manner. Sometimes it was necessary to improvise.

During my time as a Beat Duty Officer, I became involved with a course to teach basic self-defence to female members of the public. It evolved from work done by the singer Lyndsey de Paul, who lived in the area. In 1992 she developed a self-defence video called "Taking Control", which was endorsed by the then President of the Police Association, Brian Mackenzie. He noted what a positive contribution to crime prevention and the protection of women it was. The germ of an idea formed amongst a group of Battersea officers to develop and run a course for females living and working on the borough.

They devised a course to run on a weekly basis for six weeks, teaching practical moves to show how to release yourself from someone grabbing your wrist, your arm, someone trying to strangle you from the front and from the rear. A number of strikes that the students could employ using their palm heels, elbows, knees and kicking. Neatly wrapped up in the classes were some thoughtful; and considered handouts containing advice on how to minimise risk to themselves when going about their daily lives. It was crime prevention and self-preservation wrapped up into a neat little hand out, which we would discuss during the class.

The physical stuff would build to a final test for our lady students to have a go at employing everything they had remembered into a one-minute session against an instructor wearing a padded suit. The suit was a selection of thickly padded bits that you strapped to every part of your body. Made by a company called Fistgear, the FIST suit provided adequate protection to the instructor for our students to really let rip with as much force as they could when attacked or threatened by the person wearing the padding.

Our first course took place at a community centre on the Doddington Estate. My memory of it was that we were a bit nervous in our delivery and it took a few weeks for us to get into our stride. By the time we came to the end of that first course, we had received praise from the students and a national newspaper report, supporting our endeavours. As time went on we ran many of these courses and were able to fine tune the content and became much more professional with our delivery.

It was about this time the Job itself got serious about the safety of officers and the plans were put in place to update the level of training received by officers patrolling the streets. By now we had switched from truncheons to long rubber handled polymer batons and the handcuffs had changed from the traditional bracelets connected by a chain to a rigid style of cuff, that had a myriad of more possibilities. There was also the introduction of the gravity friction lock baton (made by ASP).

The course was developed as society was developing. There were more officers being injured in the line of duty. Suspects and the public at large were more inclined to resist arrest and had less inhibitions about striking officers. The police had also been on the receiving end of some adverse publicity about the frequency of deaths in custody of suspects. One of the main causes of death was positional asphyxia. A common condition for males with a large or distended beer gut. If someone like this is placed face down on the floor their gut is displaced up into their diaphragm and it can't bring air into the lungs and the person on the ground literally can't breathe. There had been a number of suspects who had died as a result of this. The Officer Safety module covered prisoner and suspect welfare, so that once a degree of control had been gained or regained, then efforts were made to ensure that the suspect could breathe and was transported as safely as possible.

The course also dealt with something that should have been obvious in an ever more aggressive and violent world which was working as a pair, employing contact and cover tactics. One officer to take the lead and interact and engage with the suspect or member of the public, while he is being covered by his colleague, who is watching from a stand-off position to deal with any signs of resistance, weapons and possibly anything trying to be discarded by the person stopped. It all sounds extremely obvious and basic, until you factor in manning levels reducing and management not wanting two of their resources deployed together.

Patrolling in pairs worked. You were more likely to deal with things as you confronted them as a pair. You were much less likely to get injured as a pair. But as the years since this Officer Safety plan was put in place, the ever-diminishing number of officers on the streets has made it very rare for officers to be deployed in pairs.

The Officer Safety training helped in the understanding of targeted strikes to a suspect. The assessed application of force to muscle groups, then joints, avoiding more vital areas in the first instance, like the head or "nads'. It minimised the risk of serious injury to suspects and maximised the number of officers who go home at the end of their shift. Palm heel strikes, use of elbows and knees. Sweeping kicks to the upper leg and toe punts to the shins and that area at the bottom of the leg, where the foot joins.

Then, using the batons to hit upper arms and legs. A back-hand strike to create distance between you and any potential assailant. The course was designed to be as basic as possible. Like me, my colleagues were not Ninja's either, so keeping it memorable and simple was paramount. That was until it came to the rigid, or Kwik cuffs, as they were known. When the course was first structured there must have been well over twenty different and complicated ways of applying the cuffs. It was clearly too much information and gradually the moves and manoeuvres were reduced to four simple styles.

We had a couple of pneumonics that were dreamt up for the course. CUT is one that I recall, to be used if faced with someone threatening you with a knife.

C- Create distance between you and any potential assailant.

U- Use cover, i.e. get something between you and the attacker. (Like Hampshire, perhaps?)

T – Transmit on your radio or mobile phone for help.

At the time of the Officer Safety update, there was so much else going on with the Job. Changes to our entire working practices as the Relief model of working was replaced with the next thing. I say the next thing because I can't really remember what came next, as the changes sometimes happened so frequently and really didn't enhance our service to the public (IMHO).

Then the uniform started changing. It was a gradual thing. The tunic stopped being worn in favour of a NATO style navy jumper with epaulettes. This was teamed with a new overcoat to replace the much-maligned long raincoat I'd been wearing and grumbling about since 1485, sorry 1986! The new jacket was allegedly made of Gortex, so waterproof. Hmm! I was never sure it was genuinely Gortex. It was also designed with a big open V at the front, so you could still see the tie. That was tickety boo until it rained and the front V of your jumper and shirt got wet. I was not on the beat when the trousers were replaced by ones made from a more durable and practical material. Then we got into the whole body-armour thing.

The first incarnation of the stab vest was designed to be worn under your shirt. It had Kevlar sheets slipped into a cotton cover, which tucked into your trousers. Your shirt and tie were worn over the top. We were given about five or six covers so you could wash them and have a clean cover every day for duty. I have to suspect it was designed by someone who had never actually been a Beat Duty Police Officer. It didn't last long. Everyone needed a larger shirt, larger jumper, coat etc. By the time I had all my kit on over the top of the stab proof vest I looked like the Pillsbury dough boy and felt I might just topple over.

Next on the kit list was a utility belt to start putting all your bit and pieces on. The leather belt issued which was used primarily to keep your trousers up, was not up to the task of supporting all the new bits of kit. Plus, more enterprising officers were adding to the already weighty belt with pouches for notebooks, pen holders, Leatherman cases. I was just at the stage of considering putting my underpants outside my trousers and shouting 'Batman!' when I spotted the kit winner.

I was in the canteen with a few colleagues having refs when some 'rufty tufties' wandered in from firearms. Now we are talking kit!

Pockets bulging on every part of them. One chap had a trouser pocket that was so stuffed with things that I did think it might just be an inflatable pocket, designed to make him look busy. However, it was the last chap in the line who was my winner. He had his bullet proof vest on, with plasti-cuffs dangling. He even had a little pair of pliers, for snipping the plasti-cuffs off with, I presumed. I bet he had kit on he'd forgotten about. We then hit on a new game.

The canteen at Battersea was designed with a serving area on the left as you walked in, with all the tables and chairs arranged in front of this. When you entered, you were visible to everyone. Our game was to take it in turns to go up to the serving area behind the last of the firearms chaps, on the pretext of getting a clean spoon, napkin or something and in reality, see if you could hook anything on to the kit monster's belt. If memory serves we managed to hook a teaspoon, two sugar sachets and a laminated menu to him. Much like the game of 'Buckaroo', which we had based the idea of our game on. Eventually he noticed and was not amused as he exploded and removed the additional components of the canteen we had added to his kit. They stayed and had a cup of tea but drank it fairly quickly. We didn't see that particular crew again.

The modern-day police uniform is so much better suited to the tasks that current serving officers are faced with on a daily basis. It would probably have been useful in my day too, but part of me wonders if we, as police, have lost something by moving away from the tradition and smartness of the Beat Duty uniform I started with in 1986. An officer wearing a smart jacket, with a crisp, clean white shirt and tie underneath, neatly pressed trousers and polished shoes or boots.

It must be about finding a balance. Part of being a copper is being respected. Part of that, in my opinion, is that you have to look the part. I understand the need for change in our modern world and sadly the 'Dixon of Dock Green' image of the police officer is consigned to history. I just find that a little bit sad. The uniformed officer when I joined was expected to have a smart haircut and although tattoos were allowed, they should not be visible when wearing your uniform. As a police officer I always believed I was held to a higher standard. I was a person of more than reasonable firmness, to be relied upon in a crisis. I policed a community, but I wasn't and did not want to be part of that community. I appreciate the points of view of others; I just don't sometimes agree with what they say.

Officer Safety is vitally important and training should be encouraged. Fitness is at the core of helping officers survive on the streets. Time must continue to be given to ensure all front line, Beat Duty Officers are supported in maintaining fitness and receiving adequate Officer Safety training.

And finally.........Trinity Road

Early Turn and I am driving the Area Car.
Whisky One is out on patrol.
My operator is new, but he is a star.
The prime Divisional response is our role.

The day before we answered a shout.
'Suspects On' at flats in Fawcett Place.
Plenty of 'Bugle'; still inside, no doubt.
He's hiding behind the sofa, no need to chase.

That fateful day, we were on Cloud Nine.
Let's get another one in the 'bin' today.
We took a shout, while in Burntwood Lane.
Flying North up Trinity Road, traffics ok.

Into three lanes, as we ghost past some traffic.
Scream down into the underpass, limited vision.
Crest the hill. Three lanes, cars static!
"Oh Shit!" Hit the brakes. But a monumental collision.

We come to a stop, fortunately both uninjured.
I'd smashed into a queue of rush hour commuter cars.
The traffic skipper counted nine that I'd damaged.
The Ego dented. My light dimmed among the Class One stars.

If I am remembered for anything about my years at Battersea as a Beat Duty Officer, it will be for the minor, damage only accident I had on Trinity Road in Wandsworth! The level of carnage was immense and the amusement caused, remains to this day. Before I go into detail and vainly try and serve up a selection of poorly written factors in mitigation, I would like to express here, that this one was TOTALLY and UTTERLY down to me! As if any of my colleagues and friends didn't know already.

When I used to get posted driving Whisky One it was always such a boon to get a keen and motivated operator, who I just knew could hold his or her own as situations arose. My operator on the day of this minor dink was just such a person.

The day before I drove myself into police car-crash folklore, we had been patrolling another quiet Early Turn. It should be noted that the ground was suffering from a spate of daytime burglaries, where the suspects had clearly identified empty houses or flats, before smashing their way in and stealing property. On this particular morning, we were just emerging from punting around Spencer Park, having driven past the location of the 1988 Clapham rail crash.

"Whisky One, all units, believed suspects on, at 1 Fawcett Close."

"Whisky One, on way", yep, we'll have some of that!

(I know I say Fawcett Place in the poem, but I was struggling to find a word to rhyme with Close, so used Place instead.)

We sped down Spencer Park to the lights, through the lights and right on to Trinity Road, where it's a three-lane carriageway. Battersea is a small ground and Trinity Road is the only bit of road on the whole ground where you can get a bit of a shift on. We hammered down through the underpass and crested the rise, just about on the deck. No traffic ahead as we tore down the hill to the Wandsworth roundabout. There was a little early morning dampness to the road surface, enough to get the rear-wheel drive, Ford Sierra to drift partway round the roundabout as we took the third exit into York Road.

We hacked along York Road to just before the junction with Plough Road.

"Kill the noise!" My operator immediately turned off the Met sound siren, leaving just the blues going as we continued at a lick along York Road, with the flats coming up on our right after the Lombard Road junction. I knew that if the fire gate was closed we would have to continue all the way to Falcon Road, turn right there, then right into Ingrave street, follow that through the Winstanley Estate, before eventually reaching Fawcett Close, by which time I would expect any self-respecting burglar to be across town.

Thankfully the fire gate was open! We slewed across York Road, through the fire gate and came to a sudden halt outside number one Fawcett Close, the ground floor flat. As it was on the ground floor it had its own front door on to the street, rather than a communal entrance to negotiate first.

We are both out of the car and through the insecure front door in a trice. My 'oppo' heads to the kitchen and bedrooms, while I take the lounge. We were there in the blink of an eye, they must still be here! As I cautiously creep into the lounge, stick drawn, this chap pops up from behind the sofa and just sort of puts his hands up in a "it's a fair cop" type stance.

Normally on the Area Car, the driver does the driving and the operator does pretty much everything else, but for some reason that day I fancied going on the sheet for this one.

The scene in *Monty Python's Life of Brian* when John Cleese' Centurion arrests Brian, sprang to mind.

"*You're fucking nicked, me old beauty*", is what I should have said, but I just sort of shrugged at the villain, turned him round, cuffed him, told him he was under arrest and delivered a caution. When my mate came into the lounge he was more than a little crestfallen to see that I had decided to arrest this chap. I think he was looking for a decent body for his record of work and was a little surprised I had taken this burglar. I can't really remember why I nicked him, probably because I found him and maybe I had a board for something or other coming up and I was looking for something tangible to talk about, rather than just punting the Area Car around Battersea. Anyway, my prisoner!

Aside from his minor chagrin, we radioed back to Battersea that we had one in custody for burglary. It was by any standards, a good result. It was rare to get to the scene of a burglary quick enough for the 'scrote' to still be on premises. He was a well-known villain, so as we escorted him back to the station in the rear of the motor we were both buzzing from our success. Plenty of pats on the back from our uniform colleagues and even a hint of a smile from CID.

We finished that shift still high on the adrenaline rush of getting to a scene quick enough to get a result. It set us up as we headed out of the Nick at the end of the day and we both looked forward to another cracking day on the car the following morning.

The next day and an almost identical day in every respect. The same two of us on the car, the same weather, the same Duty Officer and colleagues working. The only factor different and completely unknown to me, were the traffic conditions in and around the one-way system in Wandsworth, leading up to Wandsworth Bridge roundabout. A road was apparently closed, causing chaos and jams for commuters trying to go north over Wandsworth Bridge. Enterprising drivers had snuck out of the jam and were using the back streets to get up on to the South Circular and then using the slip road down on to Trinity Road, to try and negotiate the roundabout that way. Remember that.

We had our usual tea and toast at the start of that shift and were still receiving glowing praise for our excellent collar the day before. Then out on our ground, no calls to attend as yet, just out on patrol. I had a bit of a habit when I drove the Area Car, where I would head to the Southernmost point of the ground, quickly. Then I could have a slow trawl up through some of the minor streets, as we gradually patrolled North, back towards the river. A simple enough plan, but sometimes you just follow a routine.

I am pretty sure that this was all part of the problem. I had formed a routine in my mind and as a consequence, I was just dealing with things using a large amount of assumption in how I reacted to situations. And you know what they say about assumption?

I drove down The Avenue, to the bottom end and turned right on to The High Road, then right again into Nightingale Lane. We had got as far as the lights in Bellevue Road at the junction with St. James' Drive when the call came in. It was an audible alarm up near Vicarage Crescent or possibly Battersea Church Road.

"Whisky One". We took the call and my operator flicked all the switches. There was a queue of traffic along Bellevue, as usual, but I off-sided the lot, thanks to a bus that blocked all the traffic coming towards us as we got to the bottom end of Trinity Road. We turned right and I accelerated, heading North. This part of the road is a single carriageway section, one lane in each direction. Traffic was heavy but it was moving, so I made progress with some timed overtakes and a little restraint when necessary.

You get in the groove as you drive with sirens blaring and blue lights flashing. I had hunkered myself down in my seat and felt like I was on it. I could feel that my operator was in a similar state of readiness and possibly anticipation for another decent result. There was also a little déjà-vu, as we hurtled up Trinity Road, now with Wandsworth prison on our left. This was exactly the same time and location as when we had taken the burglar shout the previous day. I got past all the stationary traffic at the lights by the prison. We now have three lanes empty of all traffic in front of us and I press the right pedal to the carpet.

One of the most obvious and earliest rules we were taught on all my driving courses, was that you should always be able to stop in the distance you can see to be clear. As I screamed down Trinity Road towards the underpass, you pretty much lose all vision and consequently, I should have bled-off much of my speed until my vision came back as I crested the rise the other side of the underpass. But I made an assumption! I was using yesterday's experience at that location, at this time, and as I had NEVER seen traffic backed up in Trinity Road here, I kept the speed on.

I crested the rise.

"Oh Shit!" as I saw three lanes of stationary traffic backed up from the clogged roundabout. I braked, cadence braked too, but I was carrying too much speed and all I could do was aim for a gap between the offside traffic and the middle lane traffic. We therefore entered this narrow gap and widened it with the car, smashing wing mirrors and door panels as we careered on. About four cars into the jam, a car was straddling the lanes. It was this car that finally brought us to a stop.

"Probably turn the noise and the lights off now. Are you ok?" I turned to my operator, who looked ok.

"Yeah, I'm fine, you alright?" he kindly asked. I was uninjured physically, but my pride was more than a little dented.

"Whisky Alpha receiving Whisky One, over".

"Whisky One, go ahead, over.

"We've had an accident in Trinity Road, about 100 or so yards South of York Road Roundabout, over"

"Received by Whisky Alpha, any one injured, over?"

"Err! Hard to tell at the moment, better get an ambulance to the scene, some officers to help with traffic and better get a garage skipper (Traffic Sergeant / Black Rat), over".

"Whisky Alpha, received. How many vehicles involved, over?"

"Stand by, over". By this stage I was out of the car and checking on the condition of all the members of the public, whose cars we had smashed into. I looked around counting the cars.

"Whisky Alpha, receiving, 902, over."

"Go ahead, over".

"Yes, nine vehicles, over".

"NINE! Sorry can you confirm, Whisky Alpha, over". The incredulity in his voice made me smile.

"Yes, nine, one less than ten, over".

"Received".

This confirmation of the magnitude of my, minor damage only, accident acted like a magnet to the rest of my colleagues on duty, not just on Battersea's ground, but pretty much anyone working in South London that morning. If the boot had been on the other foot and I had been listening and heard that one of my mates had been involved in such an incident, I would have made my way to the scene too!

In the first instance my colleagues were brilliant, making sure that both my operator and I were uninjured and that all the public involved were ok, too. Then the piss taking started. You just have to go with it. Some officers had clearly turned up for a gloat, to see the Area Car driver brought down a peg or too. That's fine and just as it should be. With the benefit of hindsight, it was a long time coming. I probably needed to have my ego dented and for my driving to slow down a bit.

I was perched against the dented bonnet of the Area Car when the Traffic Sergeant turned up to start his investigation. They do have a reputation for being officious wankers, but to his credit, this chap reigned in his criticism to my face to just a couple of sharp intakes of breath as he listened to my recollection of events and surveyed the damage. We were by now, also joined by several helicopters in the sky, which I subsequently found out were a couple of radio station 'Eyes in the Sky', reporting how the 'Boys in Blue' had exacerbated the traffic carnage that morning, bringing the whole of South London to a standstill.

Several other Traffic Officers were now on scene, marking the positions of all the vehicles involved with their brightly coloured markers (cosmic crayons). I was wide eyed as an officer marked a wheel position about four feet up a concrete parapet. There were literally wrecked cars everywhere. I was formally suspended from all driving duties and got a lift back to the Nick in the back of the van. Oh, how the mighty have fallen!

During a chat with my Sergeant, he suggested perhaps taking a couple of days off sick. Albeit I knew I wasn't injured, it was an excellent suggestion and an opportunity to have a think about what I was going to do now. The suggestion was also put to my young operator that he might want to take a few days off too. It might look better for me if he did, if there was any disciplinary board in the future.

What was I going to do now then? I returned to work the following week and sat down again with my reporting Sergeant. He was a terrific chap, loads of experience and quite a benevolent attitude towards me. Considering I could be a cantankerous and obtuse git, it was something of a surprise and made me feel so much better. We discussed a few options. Stay on the team, doing shifts, but I would be open to just about every shit duty and aid commitment going, so that wasn't attractive. How about a Home Beat? That didn't initially appeal either, but then I started thinking about it more, as I sat in his office with a coffee.

Come off the shift pattern. No more Nights for a while after doing them continuously for nearly nine years. Work unsupervised, attend community meetings and decide what hours you do, so the needs of the Home Beat can be met. Avoid most aid and other shit postings that I was now in play for, as a non-driver. Where do I sign?

I became the Home Beat for the Doddington and Rollo Estate. A tightly compacted selection of tower blocks, many of them linked by aerial walkways. Not so much a community, as a selection of vertical villages. I used to patrol mostly inside the various blocks and used the walkways between them. I got to know the shop keepers, the pub landlords and the religious leaders. I knew many of the faces moving through the area and got quite good at spotting wronguns for my colleagues to turn over. All of this helped to distract me from the very real concern, which was my driving future.

Uppermost in my mind was the likely penalty or punishment I was going to get for my 'Wacky Races' style parking in Trinity Road. If you recall, I had been involved with the collision with the Citroen 2CV when driving the van and ended up gripping the rail, so I was primarily worried about receiving a summons for something like Dangerous Driving. Naturally the investigation when you smash into nine other motor vehicles takes its time. It was at least six months and I had heard nothing. If it had been dealt with the by the Process Section clerks at Battersea I could have gone in there and asked, but Wandsworth Police Station Process Section were dealing with it, so it was more difficult for me to enquire.

I had given my statement. I put my hands up as being responsible for the collision. I would have had to be some sort of miracle worker to talk my way out of that. Then the word got back to me. There were NO witnesses to the incident. As I had come flying down Trinity Road from the lights up by Wandsworth Prison, I was far ahead of the following traffic. I was up and over the rise, out of their sight at the point of the crash. None of them saw what happened. In a similar vein, all the stationary traffic in front of me were facing North, waiting their turn to negotiate the roundabout in the traffic queue. None of them saw me hurtling towards them from the rear. They all felt the impact and subsequently had seen the utter carnage and devastation, but none of them witnessed the actual smash. Somehow that seemed to work in my favour.

I don't know if the Process Section at Wandsworth were scratching their heads as to how to proceed, but there is a limit on the time they had to dream up what to do with me. It may well have been that due to the unique set of circumstances the time had just elapsed. This then explained why after about eight months, I was informed that no further action would be taken against me for the not inconsiderable damage only accident I had caused.

Phew! Knowing the Job as I do, that has to be considered a major turn-up of events. All I had to do now was try and regain my driving classification.

Several weeks after the No Further Action result, I got word that I had been allocated a check test back up at the Hendon Driving school. It would be conducted over one day and I would have to demonstrate to an examiner that I still retained all the qualities expected of an advanced driver. I elected to drive my own car up to Colindale and park at the school. The vagaries of the public transport network were too much to risk being late for such an important day. It also meant I could travel in half blues and lay the rest of my uniform on the back seat, rather than stuff it in a bag. I wanted to make a good impression and my shoes were polished like glass, my hair was neatly trimmed and I was freshly shaved. Standards!

My examiner met me in the canteen and he was relatively young for such a position. That was another relief, someone young, rather than some crusty old fucker, who can't remember the last time he drove a police car in anger! We had a good chat about my driving history. He also discussed his own journey to the position he currently held. He had recent street experience and seemed to empathise with my own circumstances. We went through what he was looking for that day. Show him a good, safe and systematic drive, but he was also looking for some flair and finesse. Don't be too safe, that's no way to pass either. I was getting the message. It may have helped my cause that I was completely open and honest about the paint scrape in Trinity Road and gave an account of it in a matter of fact and open way.

Into the car and for the life of me, as I write this, I can't remember what make and model it was. Probably something with a bit of poke. At that time, the Metropolitan Police were going through a period of examination into the cars that we were using. Most weeks at Battersea a new car would turn up for us to destroy (test drive). We got the death knell vehicles from Leyland; The Montego and then the Maestro EFi. That was unbelievably quick, but didn't have any brakes, so one for me to avoid! Then we had one of the last offerings from Rover, the 220. Sad, when you consider some of the vehicles they had produced were such iconic police cars and they finished with the 220. It reminds me of something I heard on 'Top Gear'.

'A Rover, driven by people whose life is almost over!'

One of the vehicles we had before The Job went all Vauxhall for a few years was the Volkswagen Golf VR6. That was a beast and well suited to a small ground like Battersea. It would wheel spin all the time and there wasn't much room for all our kit in it. I think we were averaging about 9 miles to the gallon too, so plenty of time filling it up, but it could certainly shift.

Back to the check test. I completed a pretty good cockpit drill. I'd done plenty of revision before I got there that morning, determined to give as good an account of myself as possible. He asked me to take the car out and just drive, get a feel for the vehicle and then we could begin the test. I did wonder if we would stay in the more confined and limited roads around the driving school, but we headed out of town and into the countryside.

One of the things about driver training, is that they like you to stick to the speed limit, even when doing a test. You can be hammering along and if you flash through a 30-mph restricted section of road a little over the thirty, it's a black mark against you. Then when you get to a section of National Speed limited roads, you can 'give it some Bugle'. The National Speed limit sign is a white circle with a diagonal black stripe through it. I write this because I do sometimes wonder if motorists are aware that's what it is. In the police, the National Speed Limit signs were fondly referred to as 'GLF's (Go Like Fuck!) and that was what was expected of you; in a safe and systematic way.

The check test started with some restricted roads and I negotiated traffic and street furniture hazards, roadworks and zebra crossings. A deliberate attempt to see my restraint? We continued on to some faster roads and I nimbly got us through the traffic we encountered. Then, out on to the motorway and we got going in the outside lane before a sudden instruction to exit at the next off ramp. I plotted my route neatly across the carriageways and was able to do a fast, safe exit from the motorway. The whole experience lasted about an hour, with full commentary on my drive throughout. It was a tough hour and despite it not being that warm a day, I was sweating as he asked me to return us in a more sedentary way to the Driving School.

He bought me a coffee in the canteen and we sat as he began to talk through my drive. This debriefing was so reminiscent of my final drive debrief at Bushey Sports Ground all those years before. I was listening, but not really. My brain was just hoping I had done enough to pass. Eventually he finished and turned his head to me.

"How much of that did you hear?", he smiled, clearly knowing my mind was elsewhere.

"You liked the exit from the motorway", I smiled back.

"It was a good drive. You demonstrated the restraint I was keen to see. You also made some good judgement calls in the traffic to facilitate our progress. The acceleration was smooth and the braking was progressive. The faster stuff on the motorway was excellent, as was your exit on to the off ramp. I have given you a mark of 91%.

I was almost in tears as he shook my hand. I know it's only a driving course, but I was proud to be an Advanced Driver and was keen to continue as one. Plus, I didn't really have that many other skills in the Job, back then.

I returned to Battersea a few days later and drifted into the office to see my Sergeant.

"Well done Guy, so I suppose I am now looking for a new Home Beat again?" and he smiled as he shook my hand.

"Thanks very much. Can I finish the month and then I'd like to return to full Beat Duties please?"

"That's fine. I'll see about getting you a posting on Whisky One with the Duties".

I smiled as I left his office and strolled into the canteen. It wasn't my Relief, but by now most people knew me and I sat down with some uniformed colleagues and talked about my recent Hendon Driving School experience. I didn't let on the result immediately.

"So, come on then. Are you still an Advanced Driver?' the question ultimately came from across the table.

I looked around the table and into the eyes of the one asking the question.

"Nah mate!.... I'm a Class One!"

902WA. Over and Out

Beat Duty coppering is hard work, incredibly varied and has its highs and lows. For the majority of the time, I loved every second of it. With the exception of one or two Inspectors, you were left alone to do the job to the best of your ability, relying on more experienced colleagues and a collection of Sergeants, whose wisdom and knowledge saw you through. It was at the beginning of my service, so maybe time has dimmed some of the memories, but the fact I still retain so much of what we did and am still friends with so many I worked with, is testament to the bond we all built during those years.

I have one or two comments to make about how things have changed since those times. My opinions are very much my own. I don't have any degrees or diplomas in psychology, policing or crime statistics, just the nine years I spent working the streets of Battersea in uniform and a total of 30 years service as a police officer.

When we were going through training at Hendon in 1986 we got to about week five and we were introduced to the Racism and Diversity package. It is probably as good a time as any to declare that I am the son of an RAF Officer and went to a private school, funded by the RAF, after my father's death in service. As a consequence, this very middle-class upbringing had rather shielded me from exposure to the range of minorities within our society. I do like to think that as such, I was a bit of a 'blank canvas' as regards my attitude towards race and the understanding of diversity. I readily listened to the training and took everything given to me on board.

Part of the week was devoted to our understanding of stereotyping and how easy and lazy it is to label people, usually through ignorance or making a poor choice. There were plenty of discussions about how we all, in society, stereotype and as a police officer, it is imperative to deal with each set of circumstances and each person you interact with on their merits, rather than forming an opinion before any engagement had taken place. It all sounded reasonable to me.

The slightly strange irony I feel, all these years later, is how just about every media outlet, every report about the police tends to stereotype the police. The dreadful circumstances surrounding the Stephen Lawrence murder ended up with an outcome that I would suggest is completely awful for everyone. No real justice for the family and an entire police force (or service) branded as institutionally racist by the Macpherson Report. I didn't work on the ground where Stephen was murdered. I have no direct knowledge of that crime, who committed it or who investigated it. I therefore have no right to comment directly on that particular case. But at some stage a report was commissioned and suddenly I, as a member of the Metropolitan Police, was labelled as Institutionally Racist. Is that not stereotyping?

From my personal perspective on policing. I just dealt with what was in front of me. I neither had the time or inclination to target any minority group. In those years I was just too busy answering calls and dealing with the work. If the perpetrator of a particular crime was described as an IC3 or IC1 then I would go hunting for someone that matched that description. Criminals too, are very quick at reading the room, as it were. If you start accusing the police of being racist or suggest that the police are targeting their stop and searches at a particular minority then the wronguns and scrotes will very quickly use this information to their advantage and if they still get caught, then declare in some way that they have only been nicked because of their ethnicity. It sows the seeds of doubt in the passers-by and then the Defence Barristers rise to their feet with some excellent words in mitigation for their client. This then spreads to the wider community, until everyone starts to believe that the police are, as an entity, racists.

I was driving Whisky One down York Road one evening at about 10pm. It was dark, with minimal street lighting. As I approached the lights with Plough Road the car in front failed to stop at a red light. Not an 'amber gambler', but a proper good red. We put the noise and lights on and crept across the junction, then tried to catch up with the offending vehicle. The vehicle was a three series BMW, with a canvas soft top roof and the rear plastic window was almost opaque in the evening light available. As my colleague was doing a vehicle check over the radio I got the car to pull over in a bus stop near to the Wandsworth Bridge roundabout. We both got out of the car and approached the now stopped BMW.

The driver leapt out of the car and came quickly towards us, which is going to make you feel a little bit threatened and on your guard.

"What the fuck! You only stopped me because I am black!"

Now this announcement was becoming more increasingly levelled at me whilst on duty, more frequently once the media and independent reports started portraying and stereotyping police in London as racists.

I informed the driver that I'd actually stopped him for running a red light. Whether he was listening to that I have no idea, as he was still circling at 50,000 feet. You just have to let people vent sometimes and my operator and I just let him run out of steam before we interjected.

I explained that it was purely a stop to bring to his attention that he had just committed a moving traffic offence and that's what I wanted to discuss with him. I had never met him before, it was dark and the interior of his car was invisible to me, so my ability to know his ethnicity was minimal, to say the least. To his credit he had started to listen. He went on to explain that it was the fourth time he had been stopped in as many days and he was fed up with it.

I attempted to continue the debate by asking what the stops had been for? One was for speeding, one for parking within the confines of a pedestrian crossing and one for doing a no left turn (not Stanmer Street!). His anger level had lowered to a warm simmer as I tried to suggest that it may have been that he was stopped because he was driving like a twat, rather than some premeditated Metropolitan Police directive to only stop black people. I continued to argue that I can only deal with what's in front of me and his committing the red-light offence meant I was duty bound to at least stop him and have a word.

By this stage we had all his particulars and my mate had quietly done a name check on him over the radio. He leans into me and whispers that the bloke is disqualified from driving.

Oh, this is going to be interesting, I thought.

I am immediately about four stages beyond the now, thinking how this might go. He perhaps cuts up rough because we arrest him and it ends up in an almighty "ding-dong" with us rolling around in the street with this black prisoner and every passing motorist sighs as they see those racist Met. coppers, at it again.

"It would appear you are disqualified from driving, sir?"

Suddenly the grandiose display of anger is replaced by silence and he stares at me, knowing the games up.

I was able to handcuff him (in an approved Home Office manner) without any histrionics and he stood quietly as we got a few other units down to search the car. We found a couple of evil looking knives in the glove box and some cannabis, but only a small personal quantity. At the end of the day, it was a chance encounter that resulted in an arrest.

The irony was that had he calmly sat in his car after we'd stopped him, the way I was policing at that time I may well have given him a verbal warning for the red light, as no danger had been caused and no one else was involved. This may have happened before my 'oppo' did a name check and we would have sent him on his way with a bollocking. Part of me wondered if he had gone into meltdown mode as some sort of defensive strategy, to make plod shy away from actually stopping him properly. When you have people behaving in this fashion it does make it rather hard to be objective about the whole race thing.

As I was continually bombarded by media reporting, independent luminaries writing reports about the police and my own stops being branded as racist it does wear you down. It makes you question yourself. Was that last stop legitimate? Did I target that individual because of his ethnicity? Have I turned into some sort of racist in this institution?

Of course not! That last stop was a bloke who matched the description of the robber to a tee, oh and he still had the lady's purse on him. The last target I was looking for was a prolific burglar, who happened to be an IC3. Wrongun's the pair of them and this had absolutely nothing to do with their ethnicity.

Policing is hard. The general public and more particularly scrotes and criminals seize upon things they see and hear. A bit of mitigation to suggest the officer was targeting a particular racial grouping. Defence councils leading with this in front of the Juvenile and Magistrate's Court muppets.

The opening up of the doors of the police to the media was, in my opinion, also a mistake. I remember The Bill coming along on ITV and dramatizing the daily goings on at Sun Hill Police Station. Individual officers in the programme becoming famous. So much so that the actor that played PC Stamp started the media ball rolling with his 'Police, Camera, Action' videos of dash cam footage from police car chases? This whetted the public's appetite for all things police, initially great PR, but the media can edit and twist things for their own agendas too.

Even comedy programmes of the time were getting in on the act. 'Not the Nine o'clock News' and later 'Alas Smith and Jones' had several very clever sketches centred on Policing. The Constable Savage sketch springs to mind and a less well know one by Mel Smith and Griff Rhys Jones.

A battered and broken police car drives into the yard in front of a senior officer.

"My God, what happened, that car was new this morning?" the senior officer turns to the driver.

"Err! Slipped in the shower sir!"

I laughed too, it's a funny line. But eventually if you keep up this constant stream of thought to the viewing public it begins to stick in the minds of some.

As time has gone on the reports and criticisms have increased. It must be hard to have the motivation, as an officer, to do anything for fear of causing offence to someone. It does seem as if the Beat Duty copper no longer has the long serving 'Old Sweats' to learn from and struggles with the daily tasks allocated. I don't know what happened with Senior Officers either. There were always one or two who could be relied upon to make a sound and rational decision and who supported their officers completely. But they do now seem very few and far between. The modern Senior Officer always appears keen to apologise, when it might be refreshing for them to defend their officers for a change.

It is though, important to mention that there are some awful police officers, who have committed the most horrendous crimes and they should never have been allowed to wear the uniform in the first place. In an any organisation the size of the police service, you are going to get the odd bad apple. Why were they allowed to serve? Was it something to do with the reduction in the standard of vetting or the general lowering of standards of entry? Did the decision-makers lose sight of what you need to know about individuals before you accept them as officers? Did the Rehabilitation of Offenders Act allow those with spent criminal convictions to apply to join the Service? How can anyone with a criminal past, no matter how ancient or minor be considered suitable to be a police officer? So, make the application and vetting process fit for purpose.

Police need to be accountable and to be able to justify their actions. But they also need to be employed separately, possibly beyond the confines of employment regulations and to have access to better legal protection in this litigious world. Because, just occasionally, members of the public lie and make up stories to suit their own agenda. It's about finding a balance to bring errant officers to justice but looking out for instances where the allegations are without merit or malicious.

I believe that when I joined, with the exception of the accelerated promotion bods, you had to have at least five year's service as a Constable before you could take the promotion exam. I am pretty sure that is no longer the case. Five years is nothing, I've had longer car chases. Geoff Boycott batted for longer. What's wrong with bringing that back? Let's get some supervisors who have actually worked the streets for a bit, before climbing the greasy pole?

But enough. It's not my fight anymore. I did my time and can't change things anyway. I had the absolute privilege to be a Beat Duty copper for a while. I worked hard sometimes, did fuck all on other occasions, made great friends for life, but ultimately, I don't miss it. As I said at the beginning, I couldn't do it today. Society and its attitude to the police is different. We do need to be careful as we run the risk of ending up with a police force (or service) that we deserve. One that is so busy self-flagellating itself for its supposed failings that it neglects to actually perform the role that it exists for.

Witness Statements

While putting these stories together I thought it would be fair and fitting to ask some of my friends and former colleagues about the time they spent as Beat Duty officers at Battersea. Below is a selection of their thoughts.

Having left home as a teenager, to live in Nightingale Lane Section House, it was a result getting posted to Battersea. On our Relief there were all sorts of characters, that you learned from and also admired.

Being so young, patrolling the streets of South London at all times of the day and night helped me grow up fast. You very quickly understood what was accepted and how to blend in and work with colleagues. They were like a second family, who I loved working with for so many reasons.

There were things of note that happened, like the Clapham rail crash and the Tottenham Riots, which I was posted to as part of a Divisional Support Unit (DSU). You had the trust, loyalty and commitment from your peers. There was full support regardless. If there were any disagreements, they were quickly settled, without any grudges kept.

There were great times on duty and off duty, with days away and drinks after work. We had so many wonderful people on our Relief.

There were the initiation 'wind ups' when we joined. It was like getting accepted. Mine was when I was told I had been contaminated with chemicals after searching an area of land in Mid-February, when we were Nights. A trip to the fire station to be tested on their machine, then hosed down by firemen in oxygen masks and others scrubbing me with brooms. I was really worried about losing my hair. Then when I reappeared from the drying room the whole Relief was there, clapping and laughing like mad. It really felt like you belonged.

There were some great jobs, some top leaders, but you learned most from the street cops with experience. There was always support when needed. It's also where a good number of us met our spouses.

All these years later, we still keep in contact and have our reunions. I'm seeing Steve tomorrow and I still remember what he drinks and his fetish for cheese!

Martin. (the young van driver, who had a sixth sense for villainy!).

In terms of working at Battersea. It was arguably the best posting of my career. I'm not sure if it was because it was my first, but it was certainly the most enjoyable. I was working with the best people, who you could trust to back you up. Even the 'gaffers' back then looked out for you.

The camaraderie and social gatherings within each Relief was brilliant. Working with your mates, then hanging out with them on your days off was satisfying.

In terms of working, it was the sheer variety that added to the challenge.

Rob.

They say your first 'Nick' will always be your favourite, which is true. Mine was Lavender Hill. But in those days gone by, Battersea and Lavender Hill were twinned together and officers and staff got to know each other well. There seemed to be a sense of belonging at Battersea. You may not have got on with all, but if you needed help on the 'hurry up' then everyone would turn out, both friend and foe.

I served at various other stations during my service. They never lived up to the sense of belonging that you had at Battersea. Would I do my time there again? Without a doubt!

Anon.

I was posted to D Relief at Lavender Hill in 1978. I was given a warm welcome and after a quiet start I began to find my feet. I loved policing and thought it was a great ground to work. It had a bit of everything.

When I was younger I think I was a little intimidated by rank. It all seemed far more disciplined back then. I loved the work and considered my colleagues to be family. There was great camaraderie.

We enjoyed functions and after work drinks were a part of our lives.

Like most things in life, I listened and learned from all the advice given. You soon sort the wheat from the chaff. I'm glad I went to a division like Battersea, being a London boy.

I always thought it was easy to balance being respectful in the right circumstances, then throwing a few 'fucks' into people on other occasions.

I think the true measure of that time is that we are all (mostly) still friends today.

I had the opportunity to do many different things throughout my career, but can honestly say I had a great laugh, never really considered it work and have absolutely no regrets. I don't think you can do better than that!

Steve. (one of the esteemed Area Car Drivers when I joined D Relief)

One thing that always stands out is the night of the 'Great Storm'. When we had occupants from some of the Mansion Houses, who had been brought into the canteen at Battersea Police Station, as a place of safety, because of damage to their properties. We shared that lasagne you had cooked for us with them!

Derek. (D Relief's Chief Mumper.)

When I was posted to Battersea, I was initially disappointed, as I would have liked to have been nearer the motorway to ease returning to my Staffordshire home. My first shift on Nights and I was posted as operator on the van. My first arrest was for an offensive weapon (a machete!). C Relief were brilliant and I can say that everyone at Battersea, even the other Reliefs were friendly and we all looked out for each other.

There were social functions put on by the social club. These would coincide with each Relief's long weekend and I recall virtually the entire Relief would turn out and make the most of it.

There were some great characters and whilst I am sure there was occasionally some discord, it never lasted long.

Simon.

I came to Battersea on IDT (Inter Divisional Transfer) with about five years in. I was supposed to be taken out and shown the ground, but they were short staffed. I was told to get out there in a panda car and do the best that I could. One of the stalwarts of the Relief took pity on me and we spent the shift together. It was a wonderful initiation and first day. There was so much warmth and friendship. We had such a good group of people on the Relief. Everyone just got on. There were one or two who were on the periphery of the main group, but even they knew someone had their back when they needed help.

It was a great ground to work, with so much going on the whole time. We had so many major incidents, that came so close together. The Marchioness, Kings Cross fire, The Clapham rail crash, there was just so much, seemingly all at once.

We worked hard, but we played hard too. There was such a wonderful social side to it all, with sponsored cycle rides to raise money for the Zeebrugge ferry disaster. We had days out and days away, loads of great parties too! Maybe we were just lucky?

Dave. (The driver of the first Area car I ever sat in.)

When I was at training school all I wanted was to be posted to Croydon. It was my home and stomping ground. But we had no say in where we got sent. I was a bit out of my depth joining the police. It would have been far more likely for me to have ended up a villain, due to where I came from. To end up being a copper was already alien and then to have the possibility of being sent to another part of London was daunting.

The day I was told my station, I was horrified. One of the only experiences of London I had was Battersea. My older siblings had taken me to the fun fair in Battersea park when I was a kid and although I have no bad memories of the fair I do recall getting off the train at Queenstown Road Station. I remember feeling that it was the most miserable and depressing place I had ever been to. Maybe it was the darkness under the bridges, but that memory of misery never left me. Whenever I drove Whisky One under those bridges, I always accelerated a bit!

Once the newness of the job faded and I got used to it, then it was like anywhere else. I did sixteen years at Battersea, gaining memories, that have only slightly faded over the years and good friends, like yourself, who will remain friends forever. Even if time and distance keep us apart.

Battersea was an amazing place to do the job we did and I would never change that. Ironically, I ended up at Croydon (because of you, Guy) and the job was much the same. But the camaraderie wasn't there. I have not spoken with a single former colleague at Croydon since the day I retired, even though I got on well with them.

My Battersea friends are a constant in my life in some way, shape or form. Even, sadly, if only at funerals these days.

Maybe there was something ethereal (if that's the right word) about Battersea. Maybe that's the reason or the denominator?

Jim. (My quarter-tipped wearing, hand grenade throwing friend).

The things I remember was being a probationer and getting all the shit jobs. Having to spend endless shifts as the Station Officer at Battersea or worse than that, Night Duty Station Officer at Lavender Hill, when you were literally the only person in the building during an eerily quiet night.

After a briefing about the theft of milk from someone's doorstep overnight. I sat watching the address, which was opposite the nick.

Along comes the suspect and I call it in. Loads of officers turned up to this startled bloke just drinking his ill-gotten gains on a wall. He was duly cautioned!

As a WPC we had the monthly stocking allowance; there were no such things as trousers for female officers when I joined, although culottes briefly appeared in 1988.

Similarly, the WPC's truncheon was smaller than the male counterpart. Light as balsa wood and about nine inches long, so they could fit into your Metropolitan Police issue handbag. They were certainly more like instruments of pleasure, than for weapons of defence or attack. We were still issued whistles. (I still have mine, dated 1910).

There was definitely a police hierarchy back then, very evident in the canteen. "Plonks should be seen and not heard", was a phrase I heard quite a lot. There were a number of "..isms", but it was normal then and only slightly aggravating to me. What I do remember is it being a much happier work place than the culture that exists today.

Terri. (The colleague and friend who published the 'crossbow incident' in Police Review magazine).

Acknowledgements

This record of my early years in the police started by accident. I was stuck at Westfield Shopping Centre in Shepherd's Bush one day in 2023. Having found a coffee shop, I got out my notebook and wrote a list of things; chores and personal admin I needed to do. Once completed, I just suddenly wrote a poem about my wife Paula, as part of a celebration for her upcoming birthday. I had a thought that it might be fun to jot down a few other poems. But what to write about?

Suddenly I had an idea. Why not put together some poems based on my time as a Beat Duty Police Officer at Battersea, from my beginnings in The Job, until I left after nine years. The first few were about the Relief and the shifts we worked. Then I recalled some of the many and various incidents and scrapes I became involved with. At the start it was just going to be the poems. But as I read, re-read and edited the poetry, I decided that each could be the start of a chapter of a fuller and more rounded story. Putting flesh on the bones of the poetry.

My thanks are, as always, firstly to my wife Paula for her continued support for all my writing. She loved her birthday poem and encouraged me to produce the twenty different poems I decided I needed to create this account. Then I presented the first draft for her to proofread. Her alterations and suggestions have made the piece flow better and I believe created a much more enjoyable and entertaining story.

Thanks once again to my cover designer, Steve Mead. He takes my ideas and runs with them and never fails to produce just the right result.

Memories are such precious things. As time passes our recollections dim a little. I have endeavoured to remember as much about my early years in the police as accurately as possible. We all have our own memories. These are just a selection of some of the incidents and moments I encountered during my time at Battersea. For any mistakes and oversights, I hope those that know and served with me can forgive. My thanks to them for their continued support and friendship.

To all who came back to me with their words about life at Battersea. Thank you for your support and the memories you sent me. There seems to be a theme running through each and every message. It echoes across the pages.

Camaraderie, friendship and complete, unqualified support for each other. I can live with that!

About the author
Guy Robin

Guy grew up on the South coast of England, near Bournemouth. He lost his father when he was five and was brought up by his mother. He was educated at Reeds School in Surrey. At 21 he joined the Metropolitan Police Service, serving for 30 years in a variety of roles and departments. His most recent work, On The Beat, describes his first nine years of service at Battersea Police Station.

Since retirement Guy worked in a variety of roles, before embarking on his writing journey. Initially the writing was a way to ease the boredom of the Covid restrictions. Guy's latest work is his third publication, following his 2022 debut, **Dysfunction** and then **Indomitable** in 2024. Guy is married to Paula and after having lived in Sussex for many years they decided to embark on a new challenge. In 2023, they moved to a small village in the Dordogne, France. They are kept busy between tending their large garden, supporting Paula's business interests and finding time for Guy to continue his writing.

Guy's interests are many and varied. He played hockey for the police and then for Crowborough Hockey club, where he and Paula met. Guy enjoys the outdoors, particularly walking great distances across the South Downs and now the numerous boucles in France. He collects stamps and Scottish Malt whisky. He is a keen motorcyclist and has become a member of a local, like-minded group. Guy has more work in the pipeline, with a new story currently in development.

Also by Guy Robin

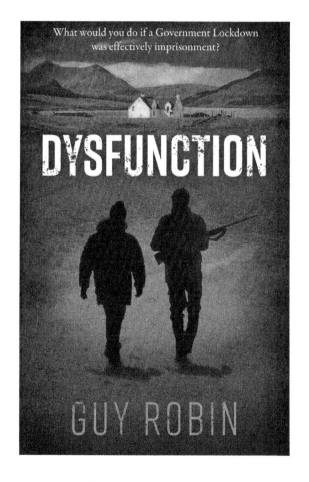

Available on AMAZON

Guy Robin's latest gripping adventure

Available on AMAZON

Printed in Great Britain
by Amazon